HANS SCHAROUN
A Monograph

HANS SCHAROUN

A Monograph

Peter Blundell Jones

Gordon Fraser
London
1978

First published 1978 by
The Gordon Fraser Gallery Ltd., London and
Bedford
Copyright © Peter Blundell Jones 1978

**British Library Cataloguing in
Publication Data**

Jones, Peter Blundell
Hans Scharoun
1. Scharoun, Hans
720′. 92′4   NA1088.S/

ISBN 0-900406-57-7

This is the second title in a series under the general
editorship of Sherban Cantacuzino. He has also
contributed the first monograph WELLS COATES.

Printed in Great Britain by
Butler & Tanner Ltd, Frome and London

Designed by Fiona MacGregor & Peter Guy

To William Lyons-Wilson

Acknowledgements

The task of investigating Scharoun's work from scratch was greatly facilitated by the existence of a catalogue of his works with periodical references. This was produced by the Berlin Arts Academy which holds a Scharoun archive, the source also of most of the drawings and many of the photographs in this book. I must therefore first acknowledge a special debt of gratitude to the Academy, to the late Peter Pfankuch and to Professor Julius Posener. I owe thanks also to Edgar Wisniewski and Peter Fromlowitz who worked with Scharoun, to Winnetou Kampmann and Ute Weström with whom I stayed in Berlin a couple of times, to Doctor August Dierks who arranged everything in connection with the German Maritime Museum, to Brigitte Wiederkehr and Cecil Deighton who helped with translations, to Gill Smith who concocted some diagrams and re-drew some plans, to Jo Bradford who typed the manuscript, and to Walter Segal, Dalibor Vesely, Dennis Sharp and Charles Jencks who gave me at various times the benefit of their opinions. Lastly, but most essentially, I must express my considerable gratitude to Margit Scharoun, who has painstakingly checked everything I have written for factual errors, and has kindly provided much valuable information and several photographs otherwise unobtainable. This book was researched and written in 1973–4.

Peter Blundell Jones

The following publishers have kindly given us permission to use their illustrations:

Posener, Julius, AA Paper No. 5: *From Schinkel to the Bauhaus*, p. 38 Mies van der Rohe photograph: London, Lund Humphries.
Joedicke, J. and Lauterbach, H., *Hugo Häring-Schriften, Entwürfe, Bauten*: Stuttgart, Karl Krämer verlag.

We also thank Horst Tappe and Reinhard Friedrich for the use of their photographs.

Contents

Hans Scharoun in 1965, photo
credit: Horst Tappe.

Introduction

In a quiet suburb of West Berlin, just above the west bank of the river Havel, one can find a tiny lane which is in most places wide enough only for a single car. It wanders lazily past a number of private houses of varied styles and sizes, each with a generous patch of garden and a thick hedge to discourage the intruding eye, then eventually peters out altogether, leading into a private garden. The lane is well lined with vegetation, and has an intimate, tranquil atmosphere. Its small scale suggests perhaps an era when the threat of the motor car was not yet taken seriously, even though some of the houses bordering it were evidently built quite recently.

At one end of this lane on the riverward side stands a modest and apparently traditional house in brick with an overhanging pitched roof. Two sides are visible from the lane: the west one which faces outwards, and the north one which can be seen from one side above the garage. The south side is quite obscured by vegetation. A casual observer walking past might remark on its being one of the older houses in the area and probably prewar, but he would continue on his way without giving it further thought, for there is nothing visible to surprise him. A keen architectural historian might be a little puzzled though by the curious disposition of the window and some of the details – like that

rather flamboyant handrail that runs up the entrance steps. Let us go inside. The front door opens into a small but adequate hall of tapering shape. We take the last door on the right and enter the living-room.

Any thoughts one had about the house being dull or ordinary are dispelled in a moment, for this room, if indeed one can call it a room, is quite startling. It feels strangely bright and open and space seems to flow this way and that with disarming fluidity,

Baensch House, Berlin-Spandau, 1935: view from road, and entrance steps

Baensch House, Berlin-Spandau, 1935. Living-room; 3 views.

unconstrained by the formal disciplines we normally associate with 'rooms'. In front of us as we enter is a vast window which appears as a gap between floor and ceiling rather than a hole in a wall, giving a strong sense of continuity with the garden. This continuity is not cut off inside the room by the centrally placed

Ground floor plan: 1, entrance hall; 2, living-room upper level; 3, living-room lower level; 4, dining area; 5, kitchen; 6, studio; 7, cloakroom and w.c.; 8, conservatory; 9, maid's room. Section opposite.

sofa for it is set into a level-change in the floor of about half a metre. The level-change divides the room into two zones, the zone between sofa and window forming the living-room proper, the space to sit about in, while the zone behind the sofa is essentially circulation space and almost serves the function of a hall, linking nearly all the ground floor elements with the stair to the first floor. Off one end of the living-room is a small circular

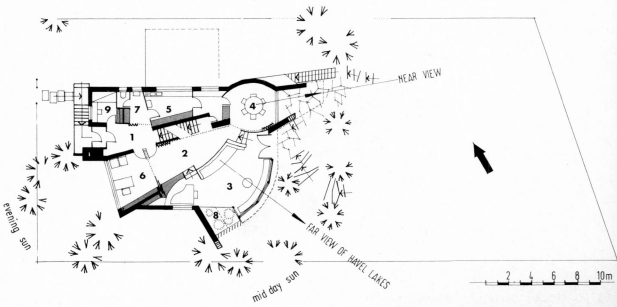

dining annexe in direct communication with the kitchen, which can be cut off visually from the main space by means of a curtain. At the other end is a small studio with a west facing window, divided off from the main space with a sliding partition. The first floor contains three bedrooms, a bathroom and a large south facing terrace in a plan arrangement which does not

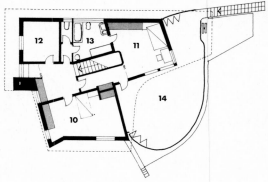

follow that of the floor below. The terrace is also accessible from the ground by an external stair.

This house was designed by Hans Scharoun in 1935 for Felix Baensch, a lawyer whose widow still occupies the first floor. It is one of the best of a series of private houses which constitute almost Scharoun's entire output during the Nazi years. All of these houses were built in traditional materials with pitched roofs and relatively ordinary street elevations, the result of restrictions imposed by the Nazi building authorities who vetoed absolutely the architectural vocabulary of the modern movement. The fact that Scharoun could

work under these conditions is significant: they would have been fatal to a Mies van der Rohe or a Gropius, whose architecture would have lost its meaning if forced into the mould of traditional construction. But Scharoun was more concerned with the spatial qualities of architecture, planning and the manipulation of

Baensch House, Berlin-Spandau, 1935. View from garden.

First floor plan;
10, 11, 12, bedrooms;
13, bathroom; 14, terrace.

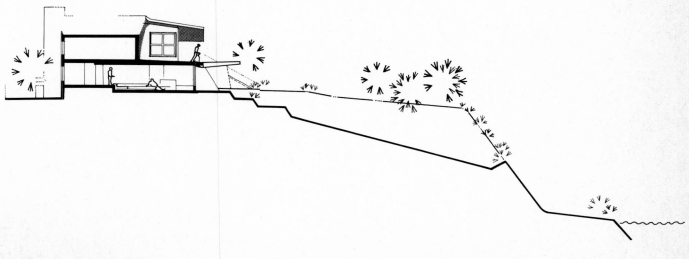

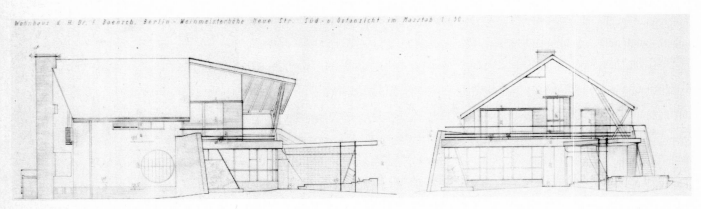

Wohnhaus d. H. Dr. E. Baensch. Berlin-Weinmeisterhöhe Neue Str. Süd- u. Ostansicht im Maasstab 1:50.

Baensch House, Berlin-Spandau, 1935: elevation drawings (not as built).
Schminke House, Löbau, Saxony, 1933; view from garden.

building elements, than with the visual image quality of buildings. He could work in almost any construction that would give him the required structural freedom. One can guess the sort of architectural vocabulary he would have employed had he not been subject to the Nazi restrictions by looking at his Schminke house of 1933, built just before the Nazi restrictions were imposed. It is a steel-framed structure with a flat roof,

finished in the customary white render of the period. One can imagine the Baensch house done in this vocabulary: the west elevation could have been more exciting probably but the essential qualities of the design, the interrelation of spaces and the relationship of building and site, would have been much the same.

Scharoun did not consider his buildings as isolated objects but as places. So rather than imposing a particular plan shape for aesthetic or constructional reasons and then dividing it up according to functional needs, as most architects do, he tried instead to allow each function to determine its particular form, and to grow his over-all plan out of the relationship between functions and site. Frank Lloyd Wright had a similar attitude: he considered that a building is a part of its site and conversely that 'the land is the simplest form of architecture'.[1] For Wright the starting-point of a house plan was the hearth, which he regarded as the heart of the conception. Having set up the hearth a shelter is needed for those who are enjoying its warmth, so a roof is added, and so on. The design gradually grows around a centre. Scharoun considered, in contrast, that with the availability of central heating the hearth had become redundant, so there is generally no single focus in his house plans. The hierarchy of functions is less clear, their interrelationships more subtle, and the whole design process is in consequence less obviously additive.

The plan form of the Baensch house did not grow out of any one element, but rather as an advantageous combination of elements. One can see that some parts have very definite shapes determined by their functions: the circular dining annexe for example designed around its table and the special corner to accommodate the piano where it does not interfere with circulation. The shapes of other parts are determined more by their inter-relation than by their separate functions and the final combination owes a great deal also to orientation and siting considerations. The position of the built-in sofa of the living-room, a fundamental plan element, was obviously determined by the view which it commands – the best view offered by the site, towards the Havel lakes. The location of the small studio was also determined by orientation – it faces westward so that the sun cannot intrude until evening and it has large windows to admit skylight during the rest of the day.

The siting of the house at the back of its plot is intended to allow best use of the garden at the front and, whereas the back is relatively hard and protective, the front of the house seems almost to disintegrate into the garden. This effect was obviously intended for Scharoun even stressed it in his details. Where the

short side wall of the dining annexe ends in the garden, for example, it does not finish abruptly in a neat edge but rather like a half demolished wall with some bricks

Baensch House; a 'disintegrating' wall on the garden side.

sticking out further than others. The level-change in the sitting-room is partly a response to siting, as it follows the natural slope of the ground and enhances the spatial continuity between living-room and garden. But it also serves to define the two zones of the living-room and to contain the sofa, almost as a happy coincidence. This kind of coincidence is something that occurs again and again in Scharoun's work. It was the kind of effect that he always sought in his planning, the solution that works well not on one count but on three or four. It gives his plans a sort of inevitability but it also makes them difficult to imitate for, though the end result is clear enough, the path by which it is gained is not evident at all. The final plan form of the Baensch house is relatively simple. It is easy to remember and to redraw yet its derivation is complex and subtle. As one examines the plan it becomes more and more evident that the fan shape was not the starting-point of the design but the end result, not an arbitrarily imposed shape but rather one discovered through a careful search of a large number of possible combinations.

[13]

Scharoun designed the Baensch house when he was forty-two and already an accomplished architect. He had built a series of highly interesting and individual buildings in the late twenties and early thirties, including a house at the Weissenhof exhibition, his celebrated apartment block at Breslau, the Siemensstadt housing development in Berlin and the Schminke house already mentioned. These four projects had been widely and internationally publicised and before the Nazis took over he had been regarded as one of Germany's most promising architects. But while they were in power he was cut off from the international architectural scene and was only able to get commissions for private houses. At the end of the war, after almost 13 years of silence, he was largely forgotten outside Germany, but he gradually re-established his international reputation and by the sixties was generally acknowledged as Germany's most eminent architect, though he is still not very widely known in the English-speaking world.

Historically Scharoun's career is of fundamental importance on two counts: firstly he was the only major architect to bridge the gap between the German architecture of the twenties and that of the postwar period, and secondly he was by far the most important exponent of *neues bauen* ('new building'), the one movement contemporary with and opposed to the International Style. However, historians generally have chosen to ignore him, regarding him as a gifted but wayward eccentric and failing to see the historical relevance of his work. One of the main reasons for this is that the critical categories set up by earlier 20th-century critics and still in general use cannot meaningfully be applied to Scharoun's work. The 20th-century historians' favourite polemic of Expressionism versus Functionalism/Rationalism is a case in point. Scharoun produced numerous buildings of an undeniably expressive character and was also an important participant in the so-called Expressionist movement. But on the other hand all this expression was intimately related to function, was, arguably, the result of function, so he ends up in both camps simultaneously as a sort of expressive Functionalist making nonsense of the polemic.

Thus Scharoun's accommodation into the history of modern architecture is no easy matter, as it requires much re-interpretation of old material and the linking together of historical strands previously considered unconnected. Because of the complexity of this operation and because most English readers will not be familiar with the work of Scharoun or the theory of 'new building' I have chosen to begin this book with a docu-

mentation of buildings, leaving historical theory until later. The first part consists of descriptions and analyses of a selection of the postwar buildings arranged according to building type, which is followed in the next part by a biographical and chronological study. I have arranged the material this way round so that readers will have some idea of Scharoun's achievements before they investigate his early life, and it has also given me the opportunity to develop his theory of design in a gradual cumulative manner. The arrangement has its advantages and its disadvantages; it was far from being the only one possible and if some readers wish to tackle the two parts in reverse order the text should still work.

PART I
Chapter 1: The Schools

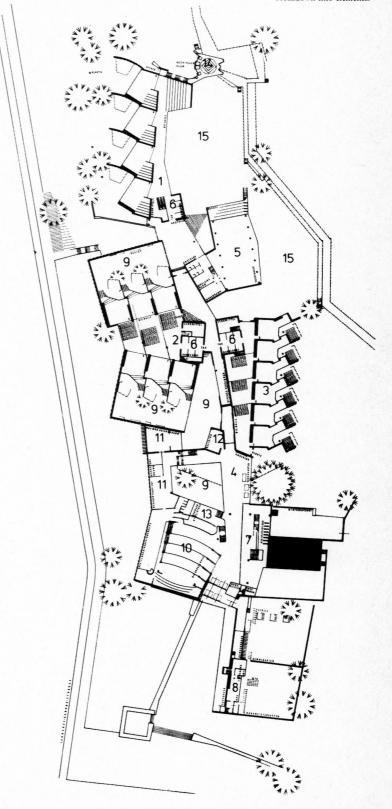

Project for a Primary School at Darmstadt, 1951. Ground floor plan; 1, upper school; 2, middle school; 3, lower school; 4, 'meeting cloister'; 5, gymnasium; 6, 'gatehouse towers' containing cloakrooms and w.c.s; 7, staff and administration; 8, porter's flat; 9, courtyards; 10, assembly hall; 11, arts and handicrafts; 12, religion; 13, library; 14, observatory; 15, playground.

Bottom left
Diagrammatic plan to show breakdown into elements.

Scharoun's three school designs provide a good starting-point for an examination of his architecture because they demonstrate, perhaps more clearly than any of his other buildings, his attitude towards formal articulation. In 1951 the town of Darmstadt invited ten architects to submit designs for various public buildings, and to take part in a conference entitled Man and Space. Scharoun presented as his project a design for a *Volkschule* (a mixed primary school) and this caused quite a sensation, for it represented a radically new departure in school design. Although it was never built, it was nonetheless widely publicised and had some exemplary effect.

A glance at the plan of the Darmstadt school project reveals a highly fragmentary building (most of which is a single-storey) on an oblong site. The plan breaks down into its constituent parts quite easily: there are three school units, upper, middle and lower school; an assembly hall with ancillary rooms; a gymnasium with

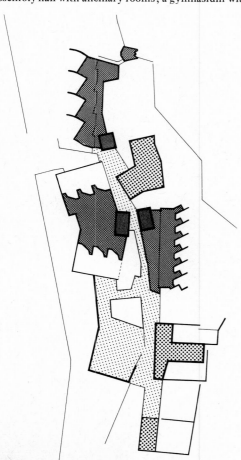

Project for a Primary School of
Darmstadt, 1951.
Plan of lower school unit;
1, 'gatehouse tower' with
cloakrooms; 2, communal space
and corridor; 3, classroom;
4, external teaching space.
Model below.

associated changing space; a four-storey administration block with caretaker's flat attached, and a curious
series of circulation spaces linking these elements. The
design of the assembly hall as a fan-shaped space with
raked seating seems logical enough, and so does that
of the gymnasium as a rectangular space with a gallery
at one end but the design of the school units, particularly the variation in classroom type, requires some
explanation.

The three school units differ in form according to
the ages of the pupils they contain, in order to accommodate the changing needs of a growing consciousness. Scharoun laid a particular emphasis on the way
in which an educational process should gradually in-
tegrate the individual into the community, making him
socially responsible without repressing his individuality. Each school unit comprises a group of classrooms
and a communal hall which serves both as circulation
space and as a meeting place. This hall is linked to the
rest of the school via a two-storey 'cloakroom tower'
containing lavatories and cloakrooms for the inhabitants of the unit. Each tower also forms a sort of gatehouse to its particular unit, defining its limits and giving it a sort of symbolic protection.

In the lower school, effectively a kindergarten,

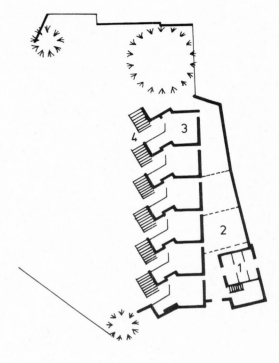

children are allowed to play a great deal, thus unconsciously developing their social awareness through being part of a group. Although at this stage they are not conscious of the quality of space, it must nevertheless welcome and protect them, thus both the classrooms and the external teaching space are small and tightly enclosed. Scharoun considered that 'physical and spiritual growth require plenty of light and sun – southlight', and therefore the classrooms of the lower school face south.

In the middle school discipline must be imposed as there is more attention to serious learning. This discipline is reflected in the planning of the middle school unit, 'space holds firm and makes firmer'. Thus the

classroom, are only half enclosed. The shared hall between the classrooms is more specialised than in the other units, having a distinct lecture/seminar area to hold events involving more than one class, rather than just an enlarged passage. The lighting condition appropriate at this stage is the 'clear light of the heavens' – northlight, and so the classrooms face north.

The three school units have very distinct boundaries and identities. Scharoun called them *Schulschaften* which can be approximately translated as 'schoolhoods' in the same sense as neighbourhoods in town planning. The space linking the school units with the rest of the school serves both as passage and as meeting place and is considered along with the assembly hall and its ancillary rooms as an 'open zone', being available for use by all pupils, whereas each school unit belongs only to the pupils of one particular group. Thus within the school there is a very definite hierarchy of privacy and space ownership which is intended to encourage pupils to identify first with the classroom and with the class as a social group, then with the school unit, then with the school, then presumably with the neighbourhood, and so on. This is all part of Scharoun's idea of integrating the child into

Left
Plan of middle school unit;
1, 'gatehouse tower' with cloakrooms; 2, communal space; 3, classroom; 4, external teaching space.

Below
Plan of upper school unit;
1, 'gatehouse tower' with cloakrooms; 2, corridor; 3, shared seminar space; 4, classroom; 5, external teaching space.

unit is formed out of two completely square enclosures and the classrooms themselves are square. Each external teaching space is shared between three classrooms and is enclosed on all sides. During this stage in the child's development direct sunlight would be distracting so the classrooms face east and west and reflected sunlight comes from the external enclosures.

In the upper school the consciousness of social responsibility is growing and imposed discipline is gradually replaced by self-discipline. The classroom form therefore becomes more open and accommodating, less rigid. The external teaching spaces, one per society by giving him a spatial network that he can experience as parallel to the social network he is involved in. At the congress of the XII Triennale in Milan in 1960, an architectural conference devoted to school buildings, Scharoun expressed his approach thus:

The most important task of education is the insertion of the individual into the community through the development of a sense of personal responsibility, in such a way that the community that results represents more than the sum total of individuals it contains. This aspect of education cannot be taught directly, it is rather a matter of general experience and the gradual formation of consciousness which allows the individual to find the right contact with public life and with the political community ... Thus a school building should not be a symbol of power politics nor primarily a product of technical or artistic perfection. Like any other building, a school should communicate an idea of a way of life sympathetic to the universal principle of democracy.[2]

The placing of the various elements of the school on its site is determined by a number of pressures. The assembly hall and administration block flank the main entrance so as to be readily available to visitors, and the three school units are placed according to orientation as previously described and with the idea of generating on the south side of the school a series of spaces for play. These spaces can also be used in conjunction with the gymnasium which is conveniently placed between the three school units. In between the entrance/administration block/assembly hall part of the school and the school units/gymnasium part there is an open courtyard with an enlarged passage to one side which Scharoun called a 'meeting cloister'. This is a part of the 'open zone' circulation space which is intended to generate informal meetings. This kind of attempt to turn circulation spaces into something more than mere passages is a recurrent feature in Scharoun's work. His buildings do not consist just of rooms and corridors but rather of a whole series of carefully modulated spaces, sometimes more open sometimes more closed. He can take a passage and by widening it, punctuating the space with a level-change and opening it up visually with a view, turn it into a meeting place. Then just as confidently he contracts it again and closes the view so it becomes once more a passage, yet the whole is one continuous space.

The Darmstadt school served as a good introduction to Scharoun's ideas about the design of educational buildings, but since it was never built it has never been practically tested and we can but imagine the quality of spaces envisaged by looking at the plan. However, many of the ideas pioneered at Darmstadt have been brought to fruition in two later designs for schools at Lünen and at Marl, both of which have been built.

The Geschwister Scholl school at Lünen, Westphalia, was designed in '56 five years after the Darmstadt project and it was built in stages between '56 and '62, being partly in use from '58. It is a secondary school for girls, taking pupils aged from ten to eighteen, and like the Darmstadt project it is divided into three units, upper, middle and lower schools. The lower and middle schools are on the ground floor, each consisting of two strings of classrooms flanking a central passage, while the upper school is on the first floor, a more exposed situation with a more extensive view, more directly connected with the outside world.

At Lünen Scharoun has dropped his specialised classroom types in favour of a more universal 'classroom unit', and this 'classroom unit' has become the

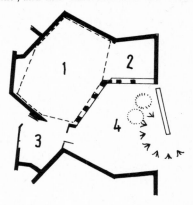

Geschwister Scholl School, Lünen, 1958–62. Plan of a classroom unit; 1, classroom proper; 2, annexe; 3, entrance/cloakroom; 4, external teaching space.

primary element of the design, the school units having become somewhat weaker. Scharoun always stressed in his educational projects the idea that the school should be a kind of second home for the child, the classroom affording him some sense of belonging and protection. In consequence he developed his classroom unit at Lünen like a small flat calling it a *Klassenwohnung* ('class-dwelling'). Each of these comprises main classroom, annexe, entrance lobby and external teaching space. The basic shape of the classroom was designed with flexibility of internal layout in mind. For the straight teaching function an essentially linear space is required in which the teacher faces his pupils but for a seminar function a circular space is more convenient. Scharoun's flattened hexagons fall between the two and can reasonably contain either arrangement. The classroom furniture is light and easily movable, and the variety of seating arrangements that one finds on a casual visit testifies to the use of this flexibility. The specific lighting orientation found in the Darmstadt classrooms has been replaced at Lünen by a more general approach. Daylighting is provided from

An external teaching space.

all sides by means of clerestory windows which provide a strong light with omnidirectional properties thus precluding problems of shadows, and there is also a window in each classroom providing a view out.

The annexe provided beside each classroom forms a space partially detached and allowing a variety of uses. Typically, it can accommodate a small group of pupils engaged on a different activity from the rest, but under the surveillance of the same teacher. The entrance lobby of the classroom unit effectively replaces the cloakroom/gatehouse structures of the Darmstadt scheme by providing coat-hanging space and washing facilities at the scale of the classroom rather than at the scale of the school unit. Each school unit does, however, have its own lavatories, but these are at the ends of their respective passages rather than forming entrances to the units as they do in the Darmstadt scheme.

Classroom shape is largely a response to internal considerations but the shapes of the annexe, lobby and external teaching space are determined also by the way in which the classrooms fit together. Thus the space left by one classroom neatly forms the lobby of the next while its annexe helps to enclose the external space of the next, and so on. This ingenious interaction of elements such that the outside of one matches the internal functions of its neighbour is one of the distinguishing features of Scharoun's planning.

The assembly hall of the Lünen school, situated once again close to the main entrance, is polygonal in shape and more suggestive of a chapter house than of a lecture hall. It is essentially a circular rather than a linear space, appropriate to the idea of democratic discussion rather than just the accommodation of a silent audience. In the Darmstadt project the pupils were too young to be expected to participate in large-scale meetings, but the girls at the Lünen school are older and

have more of an idea of social responsibility, hence a space to encourage communal discussion and a sense of community. The increased age of the pupils also necessitates some more specialised teaching rooms and there are on the north side of the building three science amphitheatres, one for each discipline, with raked seats and top lighting, separated by preparation rooms where experimental equipment can be set up.

Left. A typical classroom.

Assembly hall.

As in the Darmstadt project, the arts and handicrafts rooms at Lünen are placed near the assembly hall, but are on the first floor. The art room is a long rectangular space lit by a vast northlight studio window. It is provided with special raised galleries which allow pupils to see and draw things from a downward angle. The needlework rooms are on the other side of the first floor with south facing windows and a raised platform is

Below. Art room.

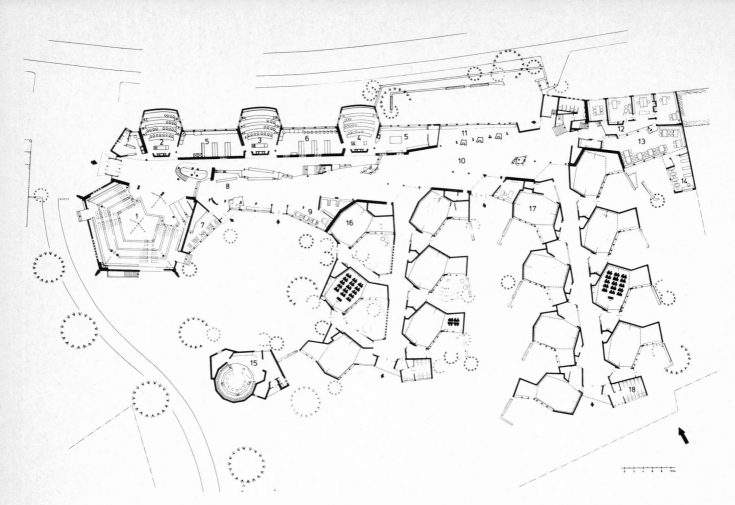

provided along the window side of the rooms which the girls use for fashion parades.

The 'meeting/cloister' idea pioneered in the Darmstadt project is even more developed at Lünen, though here it looks out on a semi-enclosed playground rather than on a courtyard and serves the more definite func-

tion of *Pausenhalle* or 'break hall', replacing the playground during wet weather. It is a more specialised space than that envisaged at Darmstadt as there is more of a clear division between what is 'break hall' and what is mere circulation space. Also it is strengthened considerably by the placing of the pupils'

Below. Geschwister Scholl
School, Lünen, 1958
Plan of first floor; 1, staircase;
2, art room; 3, handicraft rooms;
4, classrooms, upper school;
5, special classroom; 6, terrace.

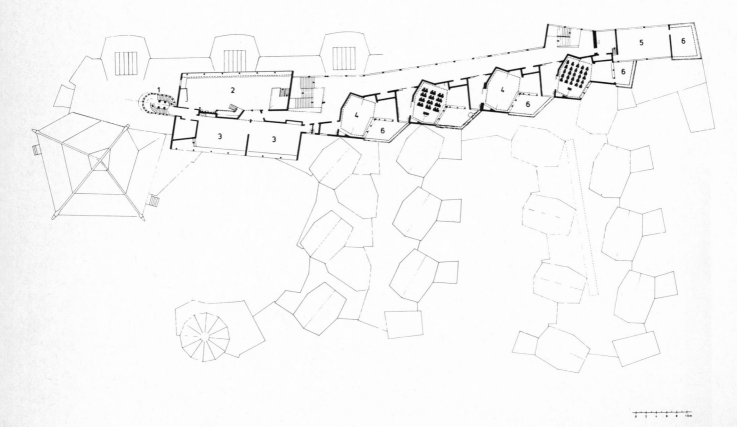

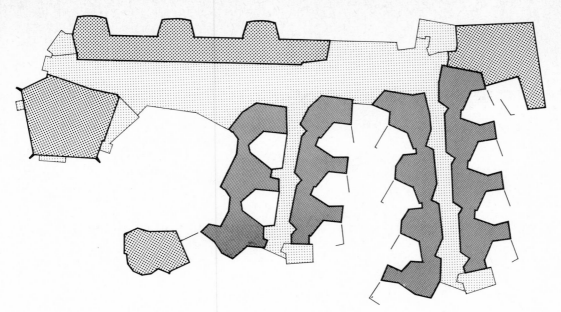

Diagrammatic plan to show
breakdown into elements.

library and common room which are deliberately made almost continuous with it, being separated from it only by glazed screens. It is an extremely complex space both to experience and in its derivation. Its overall shape is generated largely by the other more positive plan elements and their arrangement on the site. Thus it might almost be a leftover area which has been roofed in, or a courtyard internalised. Its formal sub-servience to other elements of the plan gives it a loose, open feel which makes it seem only semi-enclosed, halfway between the openness of street and the total enclosure of the classroom. Also its indefinite shape makes a strong contrast with the more positive shapes of the other parts, thus stressing its more transient function.

However, it is not just a happy accident generated by the outsides of forms around it and the circulation between elements. It is carefully controlled so that the meeting space has an adequate identity of its own. This grows initially out of the entrance passage which expands as it runs away from the main doors past the assembly hall and is then divided by a staircase. The part on the left-hand side then continues at the same level as a clearly defined passage while the part on the right expands, drops in level and is opened out spatially with a view into the playground. The small drop in level serves both to define the limits of the meeting-space area and to accommodate some built-in seating and the pupils' milk bar. The meeting space does not end abruptly as it began but tapers off as the view is lost and the passage narrows. Further down near the back door it widens out again to accommodate some fishtanks and a lesser meeting space with a view out streetwards. It is difficult with photographs to give much of an impression of the quality of this space, which depends so much on the feeling of continuity it generates. Walking through it one experiences a surprising sense of calm and ease which never occurs in more formally planned situations.

The street elevation of the Lünen school has a very

Opposite. Ground floor plan; 1, assembly hall; 2, physics; 3, biology and 4, chemistry; 5, preparation; 6, laboratory; 7, pupils' common room; 8, break hall; 9, pupils' library; 10, hall; 11, aquarium; 12 staff offices; 13, staff common room; 14, staff library; 15, music room (not built); 16, classrooms, lower school; 17, classrooms, middle school; 18, w.c.s.

Break hall

Geschwister Scholl School,
Lünen, 1958–62.
Main entrance; with assembly
hall on right, physics lecture
room to the left and art room
over.

Typical view of south side.

View from an upper school
classroom.

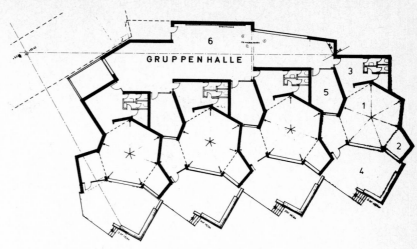

GRUPPENHALLE

6

3

5

1

2

4

UNTERSTUFE

broken up and rambling quality which makes it un-heroic in character, in keeping with Scharoun's statement that a school building should not be 'primarily a product of technical or artistic perfection'. The main entrance is conveniently placed and not at all grandiose. Scharoun's siting policy was to place the main parts of the building at the back of the plot thus allowing the classroom wings to extend out southwards into the remainder of the area, generating a series of little garden spaces. This suggests once again the idea of a building presenting a hard face to the road and then disintegrating into its site in a soft and broken manner, as with the Baensch house described in my opening chapter.

The third and last of Scharoun's school projects is a *Volkschule* at Marl, Westphalia designed in '60. It was built in stages and finally completed in '68. You will probably now be reasonably familiar with Scharoun's attitudes to the planning of schools so I need not describe this one in very great detail. Classroom units like those at Lünen form the basis of the design. These are arranged in groups of four, each group sharing a communal hall, thus setting up the kind of spatial hierarchy envisaged in the Darmstadt project though here it is not so rigorously pursued. The assembly hall gains pride of place, forming the heart of the complex and the starting point of the obviously cumulative plan. It

is of a rather more ambitious size than that of the Lünen school, being intended for use not only by the school but by the neighbourhood as well, serving as a small theatre, cinema or concert hall. To accommodate these functions it is fan-shaped in plan. This does not imply a rejection of the 'chapterhouse' principle found at Lünen, for the Marl school is a primary school

School at Marl, 1960–8. Plan of a lower school unit; 1, classroom; 2, annexe; 3, entrance lobby; 4, external teaching space; 5, courtyard; 6, communal space.

A typical classroom.

Assembly hall.

School at Marl, 1960. External view with assembly hall in centre. Ground floor plan; 1, main entrance; 2, assembly hall; 3, gymnasium; 4, lower school units; 5, middle school units (no upper school); 6, sciences; 7, workshop and handicrafts; 8, domestic science; 9, staffrooms; 10, playground; 11, seminar room.

whereas the Lünen school is a secondary school and one can scarcely expect democratic participation at a primary school level. Scharoun's intention of bringing outside life into the school also conditioned the position of the gymnasium, which is supposed to be made available to local people in the evenings and is therefore positioned at the front of the complex near the main entrance.

The location of the town of Marl in the heavily industrialised Ruhr region results in an educational bias towards technical and scientific subjects. Thus in Scharoun's school there are a number of specialised science rooms and a workshop situated prominently near the assembly hall which is designed to be like part of a factory, thus creating an atmosphere preparatory to the outside world. The school was built on an open

Main entrance and hall.

site and allowed to sprawl in all directions without the discipline and restraint of a street at one side which gave shape to the Lünen design. The result is a very fragmentary building which is virtually impossible to see as a whole in elevation. As one walks through it one experiences an endless series of rich and changing vistas and finds an immense variety of spaces, each carefully designed around its particular purpose. Almost all parts of the school are carefully daylit with windows or rooflights so that in most circumstances no artificial light is required at all.

Scharoun's three school designs demonstrate very clearly his concern with creating a building which accurately reflects his interpretation of its social and practical functions. His school plans are fragmentary in form because he wished to give an adequate identity to each part rather than to allow the parts to be smothered by the whole, as they tend to be when crammed into a single envelope. Thus he created a hierarchy of formal elements which reflects the social structure that they contain. This could be seen as deliberate metaphorical expression, but it is much more than that. He also managed to create a whole series of spaces which range in scale from the intimate to the collective and which promote social identity not just

An external teaching space.

metaphorically but from the way the spaces are experienced in practice. The building expresses its functions in the same way as a glove expresses a hand, logically and inevitably. This at any rate was Scharoun's intention. He approached a project by attempting to define what he called the 'essence' of a building, effectively the sum total of factors which make up the brief, and then to give this 'essence' material form. Of course, this process depends upon an inevitably subjective interpretation of the brief, and to that extent it is irrational, but that is a universal problem. Even if one disagrees with Scharoun's definition of the essence of a scheme one must at least respect him for his skill and consistency in giving it material form.

View from covered way between lower school units.

[25]

Chapter 2: The Theatres

We have seen how in his school at Marl Scharoun took the assembly hall as the focal point, making it the heart of his complex because it represents the whole community, and giving it a degree of architectural prominence appropriate to that function. As this assembly hall relates to the surrounding 'schoolscape' so in his architectural philosophy a theatre should relate to its townscape, representing the idea of community at a larger scale. So, although both Scharoun's built schools are unheroic in character and difficult to find, being tucked away down sidestreets and buried in vegetation, his theatre projects were all designed to be prominent landmarks, major elements in the townscape. Despite this difference of emphasis both theatres and schools are the result of the same kind of design process. We can find again in the theatres a high degree of formal articulation strictly related to the programme, and a planning policy which depends on cumulative growth.

Scharoun designed a couple of theatres, both unrealised, in the early twenties. These are youthful works which are more interesting as evidence of his development than as designs in themselves and will be considered with his other early projects in a later chapter. He did not produce any more theatre projects until 30 years later when he entered the competition for a new theatre at Kassel in '52. This project was done in collaboration with an old friend, the landscape architect Hermann Mattern, who had designed the gardens of many of the private houses which Scharoun built in the thirties. The theatrical consultant was Wilhelm Hüller. Coming just after the Darmstadt school project, the Kassel theatre project stands in relation to Scharoun's theatre projects in much the same way as the Darmstadt project does to the later schools, and the two lines of thinking run parallel.

The Kassel project was for a double theatre with large and small halls to hold 1100 and 760 people respectively. In addition there are foyers for both halls, a restaurant and three separate wings containing administrative offices, dressing rooms and scenery workshops. The focal point of the complex is the large hall, which boasts a number of innovatory features. Scharoun rejected the picture-frame stage with its proscenium arch because it provides too rigid a setting and creates too much of a barrier between actors and audience. He substituted a much wider stage which would allow more flexibility of use, as he envisaged the hall being used for a variety of purposes including concerts and opera as well as theatrical productions. He also proposed that the ceiling of the auditorium should have hinged flaps which would cut off the balcony seats when lowered, decreasing the size of the hall and improving its acoustics for small scale events. Another unusual feature was the provision of a large window at the back of the auditorium which would throw

Kassel theatre project, 1952–3. Ground floor plan; 1, main stage; 2, main auditorium; 3, main foyer; 4, small stage; 5, small auditorium; 6, second foyer; 7, backstage; 8, store; 9, dressing-room wing; 10, public w.c.s; 11, refreshment room; 12, courtyard; 13, administration wing.

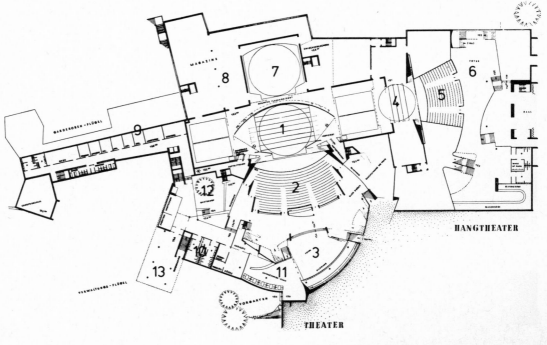

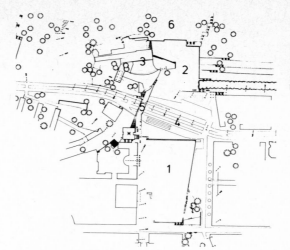

natural light onto the stage if required. The small hall projects from one side of the main stage so that the back stage areas link up. Scharoun intended that it should be built as an experimental theatre, allowing a high degree of flexibility in staging.

The layout of the complex and the disposition of its parts are determined largely by siting considerations. The building was intended to replace an old theatre destroyed in the war which had stood across the south side of Friedrichshain Square. Scharoun considered that the view from the square opened up by the demolition of the old building was worth keeping, so he sited his scheme to one side and slightly downhill of the old theatre. The slope of the ground at this point was admirably suited to the accommodation of the raked seating of the main auditorium, the orchestra pit, and the stage basement at ever decreasing levels. It also resulted in a considerable drop in level between large and small halls which was put to admirable use in the competition scheme by the formation of a roof terrace over the small hall as an external extension to the foyer of the large hall. This idea was rejected in the revised

scheme, presumably for reasons of cost.

Since the building of the original theatre the road running in front of it across the south side of the square had become a major traffic route, acting as a barrier between theatre and square. Scharoun proposed solving this problem by placing a bridge across the road directly linking the square with the theatre, and he designed the main foyer of his scheme as a link between this bridge and the main auditorium. This foyer is one of the most interesting features of the project as it can be regarded as the prototype for most of his later foyers in theatres and concert halls, including that of the Philharmonie. It is similar in some ways to the 'break hall' and 'meeting cloister' spaces which we have seen in the school designs, a space of indefinite shape determined by the interrelation of elements and the circulation between them. However, here the circulation plays the dominant role, becoming the major influence in shaping the space. The profusion of staircases and variety of levels is intended to conjure up an atmosphere appropriate to the excitement of a theatrical performance:

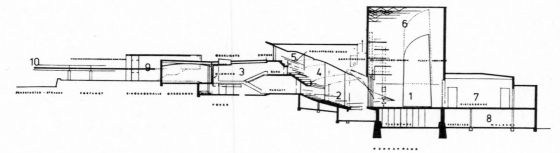

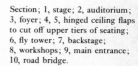

[27]

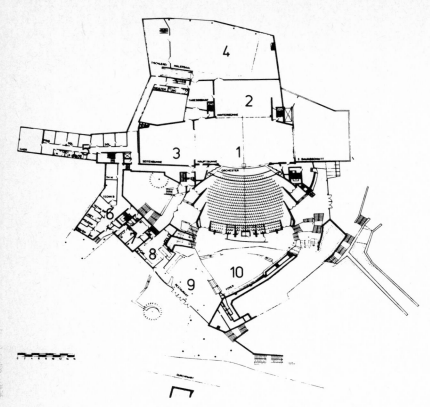

Revised ground plan 1953 (small theatre at a lower level); 1, main stage; 2, backstage; 3, side-stage; 4, workshops; 5, dressing-rooms; 6, office wing; 7, caretaker's flat; 8, kitchen; 9, restaurant; 10, foyer.

Revised plan at upper foyer level; 1, road bridge; 2, box office; 3, coats; 4, public w.c.s; 5, smoking rooms; 6, library; 7, offices; 8, dressing-rooms.

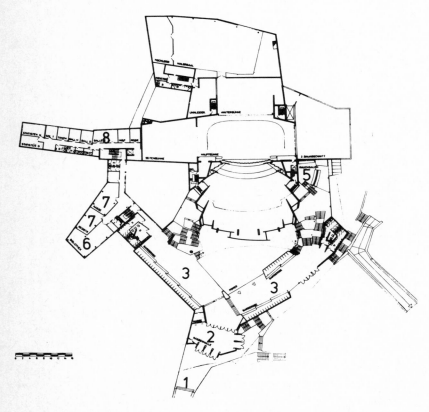

The progress of the visitor across the bridge, or from the lower approach road, through the entrance hall and cloakrooms into the auditorium is not merely a physical act, but an emotional experience. All public rooms and circulation areas, though self-contained, are visually interconnected. The circulation areas surround the core of public rooms which consist of foyer, refreshment room etc.[3]

Scharoun has a number of subtle devices through which he controls this space and the way people move through it. He often uses small changes in level to control changes of direction in circulation flow. In the upper level of the foyer one would enter the building from the bridge through the box office

then, just inside the main doors, there is a choice of direction to be made. This fact is accentuated by the stairs: one would tend to approach these straight on, having already made the necessary change in direction. In the lower level of the foyer as one walks from the restaurant to the auditorium the same choice is presented in a slightly different way, and one has to mount a couple of steps which in each case are carefully angled to halfway between the direction one comes from and the direction in which one needs to go. Another similar feature can be found in the stairs beside the main auditorium which lead down to the vomitories of the two front ranks of seats. A small landing is included in each stair near its base which allows a change in direction, so that as one leaves the stair one faces directly the doors through which one is supposed to go. The use of such devices explains to some extent that strange feeling of calm, ease and fluidity that one experiences in the circulation spaces of many of Scharoun's buildings.

Scharoun and Mattern's project for the Kassel theatre won first prize in the competition and was widely admired. It should have been built, and a revised scheme was prepared in '53. The project then dragged on but was eventually abandoned in '54 because of the client's fears concerning constructional difficulties. This was a major setback to Scharoun's career because the Kassel theatre, had it been built, would probably have brought the kind of acclaim he received after the building of the Philharmonie ten years later. This would have greatly added to his credibility and would probably have brought more real commissions between the mid-fifties and mid-sixties. The Kassel authorities did eventually commission some other architects to build a new theatre. It is very conventional in design and now looks embarrassingly dated; no doubt they regret their decision.

It is interesting to compare Scharoun's competition scheme for Kassel with the revised version. Several things are understandably cut out or reduced in size in the interests of economy, but one very curious difference is that the building becomes in its outward form more curvaceous and less angular. Scharoun wanted to make his theatre as sensitive as possible to the hilly profile of the local landscape, so he produced an undulating form which rises gently to the fly-tower dissolving it into the rest of the building. As he worked on the scheme this effect became more and more pronounced. The considerable concern with the siting of buildings and their relation to the landscape is evident in his other theatre projects, and the extreme differences between Kassel and the three later designs

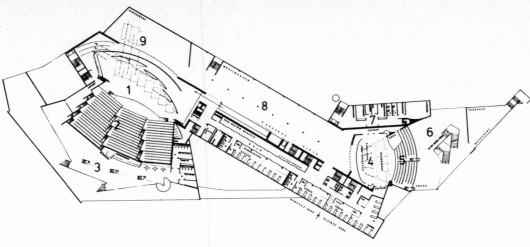

Mannheim theatre project, 1953.
Plan at auditorium level; 1, main
stage; 2, main auditorium;
3, foyer; 4, small stage; 5, small
auditorium; 6, foyer; 7, dressing-
rooms; 8, store; 9, backstage.

demonstrate clearly the extent to which Scharoun used each situation to generate a specific design rather than producing variations on the same theme.

The second theatre design was actually contemporary with the revised Kassel project. This was an entry for the Mannheim theatre competition of '53 and was awarded third prize. In preparation for his project Scharoun undertook two extensive studies, one concerned with the relation of the building with the townscape, the other with the requirements of the stage. He had always been interested in the structure of medieval towns and the hierarchy of buildings that they contained. Housing, though varied, kept to a consistent scale, whereas buildings representing spiritual values, political power or the whole community were given greater prominence both in siting and in style. Each expressed its particular function; one would not, for instance, confuse a palace with a church although both might be equally prominent. Scharoun admired the medieval town for the way in which its buildings accurately reflected the society that they contained through a direct response to function in its broadest sense. Mannheim is a city with a rich history and he made a study of its growth, noting the positions of important buildings in the townscape in order to establish a historical precedent for the siting and treatment of his scheme.

The other study, concerning the nature of various types of theatre, was undertaken with the help of Hugo Häring and Margot Aschenbrenner and presented as a theoretical paper on the architectural structure of the theatre. They argued that for some types of theatre dealing with worldly themes (like the Renaissance theatre and the French Classic) a highly ordered and disciplined stage is required, but for other types of theatre which they called 'irrational', including the open space theatre of the Greeks, the medieval mystery plays and Shakespeare, which deal with more spiritual and cosmic themes, a highly ordered theatre is a disadvantage because it constantly brings the spectator back to finite reality. This may all sound rather abstract but it leads to a very interesting and ingenious stage design. Scharoun noticed how in a conventional theatre with symmetrical seating focused on the stage and a proscenium arch over it there are plenty of scale cues and an ordered visual perspective, allowing the audience to gauge the scale and position of stage events quite accurately even without the help of cues from scenery. This limits the extent of illusion that one can create on a traditional stage, so he designed a theatre with an irregular seating pattern focused at a variety of different points on a very wide stage with no pro-

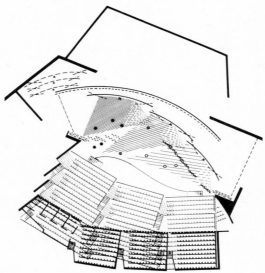

Plan of the main theatre, showing the wide stage and 'aperspective' seating layout.

scenium arch. This would make the auditorium space very difficult to assess perceptually and one would have to gauge the scale and position of stage events solely by reference to the scenery, which could be very ordered and give correct perspective cues for the 'rational' theatre or, alternatively, it could allow the use of deliberate illusions for the 'irrational' theatre. It is a fascinating idea that has yet to be tried in practice.

Like the Kassel project, the Mannheim scheme comprises a double theatre with large and small halls but the disposition of its parts is handled in a totally different manner. The two halls protrude from opposite sides and at opposite ends of a tall rectangular block containing the fly-towers of both halls linked by a mixture of offices, dressing-rooms, workshops and storage space. The site was a large square near the centre of the city, just on the edge of the old part.

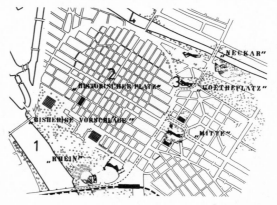

Plan of the city centre, showing possible sites for the theatre; 1, Rhine; 2, old town; 3, competition site; 4, river Neckar.

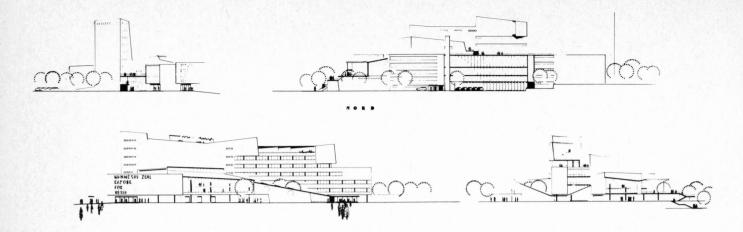

N O R D

S U E D

Mannheim theatre project, 1953.
Elevations and model.

Right. Zurich theatre project,
1964. Model.

Zurich theatre project, 1964. Plan
at auditorium level; 1, stage;
2, auditorium; 3, foyer; 4, back
and side-stage; 5, store;
6, dressing-rooms and
administration; 7, small theatre;
8, hall.

Scharoun's third and least known theatre project
was an entry for the Zurich theatre competition of '64.
It was not awarded any prize, but was nonetheless considered at the time to be worth publishing along with
the winning schemes. (First prize in the competition
went, incidentally, to Jørn Utzon, but his design has
not been built.) Scharoun was not able to pursue his
idea of a wide stage with 'aperspective' seating in his
Zurich scheme because the brief asked very specifically for a stage of normal dimensions, so he pursued
an alternative line of thought. His aim was to get away
from the flat, picture-frame stage with its almost two
dimensional quality and to bring the actors more in
contact with the audience. He produced a stage design
that could be used in the normal way with flat scenery
but which could also be used with two sets of scenery
at right angles, both set at 45° to the plane of the stage.

Rather than building parallel to the sides of the square
as most competitors chose to do, Scharoun placed only
the lower parts of his building parallel to the square,
leaving the bulk running diagonally across it but
parallel with the grid of streets in the old town nearby.
In this way the building subtly reconciles the geometry
of the old town with that of its site. The diagonal
emphasis also results in the most impressive elevations
of the building facing the corners of the square from
which it would be approached. The over-all character
of the structure is tall, compact and angular in keeping
with its dense, flat urban site and very much in contrast
with the loose curvaceous form of the Kassel design.

Thus the wings instead of being set in a straight line
with the stage are set behind it enclosing an angle of
90°. The auditorium follows this unorthodox layout
and is, surprisingly for Scharoun, completely symmetrical. The foyers are more formalised than usual
too, as the strict symmetry is followed through in the
staircases. The whole building has a rather crystalline
form which Scharoun felt was sympathetic to the surrounding townscape.

Ironically enough, the one theatre which Scharoun
was eventually able to build had to have a conventional
stage because it is for the use of visiting companies
rather than a resident company and is expected to take
scenery already made for other theatres. This is the
theatre at Wolfsburg (opened in October '73) based
on the winning entry to an architectural competition
of '65 at which Alvar Aalto and Jørn Utzon took second
and third prizes. The most outstanding quality of
Scharoun's conception was the relationship of his
building with its site. Writing generally about the

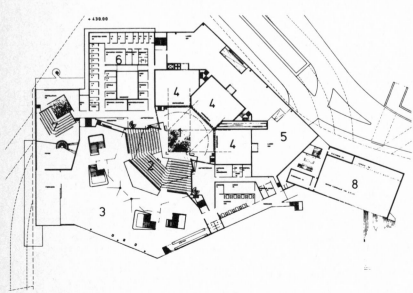

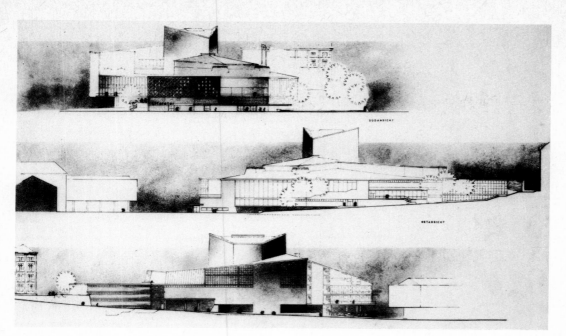

Zurich theatre project, 1964.
Elevations.

planning of community buildings in his Kassel report he had expressed his concern with siting as follows:

The planner must first take an inventory, to familiarise himself with the existing values of the landscape and to include them in his general strategy. He must take into account both existing and predicted problems and plan the townscape so that the various monuments play their correct organic roles both in relation to each other and in relation to the whole new layout. He must consider the traffic arrangements in their differentiation as being technical means at the service of form. Thus from the different starting-points the essential problems resolve themselves almost spontaneously. The technical-functional basis helps to link the given and set problems organically. The intuitive view is opened.[4]

Wolfsburg is a modern town that grew up around the Volkswagen works which remains its raison d'être. It

is a car orientated town of fairly constant density with numerous unremarkable and uniform buildings. The Porsche Strasse forms a rather weak focus as a sort of high street, strengthened a little by a monumental but uninspiring town hall and Aalto's celebrated cultural centre placed halfway along it. This is really the centre, but one does not get any strong feeling of having arrived, because the wide busy street asserts itself too strongly as a linear element with no real definition to its limits. The building of a municipal theatre afforded an opportunity to give the centre the definition that it lacked and to provide more of a sense of place, pro-

vided that the building could be sufficiently monumental and recognisably different from its neighbours, and provided that it linked both practically and visually with the existing town centre.

Just south of the town centre and to the left of the Porsche Strasse lies a low wooded hill which has been left as a green area and forms a sort of natural boundary to the town cente. The chosen site for the new theatre was the edge of this hill, running between the concert hall on one side and the Porsche Strasse on the other. This constitutes an enormous site area some way from the town hall and cultural centre which suggests a very large building if it is to make a strong enough impact. For most entrants in the theatre competition the site proved too large and their compact little theatres sat at one end or the other rather unhappily. This left most of the space quite uncontrolled and failed to produce an effect adequately monumental to dominate the space between theatre and town hall, thus failing also to keep the centre of the town as one coherent unit. Scharoun alone had the idea of extending his theatre into an immense linear building stretching right across the site to produce an impressive large scale elevation using the trees as a backdrop. This seemed unquestionably the best solution, perhaps the only really convincing solution.

Left
Wolfsburg theatre, 1965–73.
Plan of Wolfsburg; A, theatre;
B, Stadthalle; C, Cultural Centre
by Alvar Aalto; D, town hall;
E, Volkswagen works.

Site plan; 1, Porschestrasse;
2, Stadthalle; 3, wooded hillside;
4, car approach; 5, car park;
6, pedestrian approach; 7, theatre
foyer; 8, theatre proper;
9, dressing-rooms; 10, open air
stage.

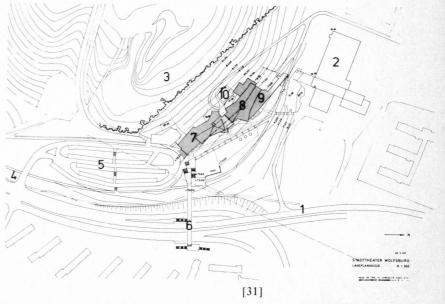

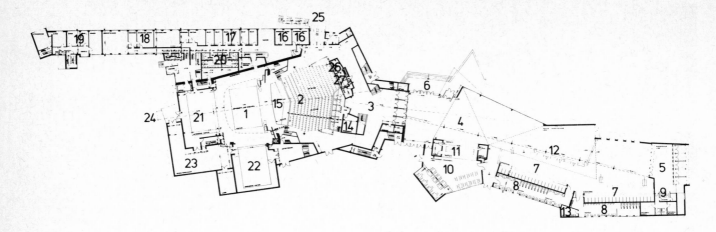

Wolfsburg theatre, 1965-73.
Ground floor plan; 1, stage;
2, lower part of auditorium;
3, inner foyer; 4, main foyer;
5, principal entrance; 6, secondary
entrance; 7, coats; 8, public w.c.s;
9, box office; 10, restaurant;
11, servery; 12, level change with
seating; 13, plant room; 14, box
for special guests; 15, orchestra
pit; 16, dressing-rooms;
17, personal dressing-rooms;
18, administration; 19, porter's
flat; 20, washrooms;
21, backstage; 22, side-stage;
23, scenery store; 24, goods
entrance; 25, artists' entrance;
26, sound control; 27, lighting
control.

Section; 1, stage; 2, auditorium;
3, inner foyer; 4, fly tower;
5, backstage; 6, goods entrance;
7, orchestra pit; 8, outer foyer;
9, plant room; 10, double window.

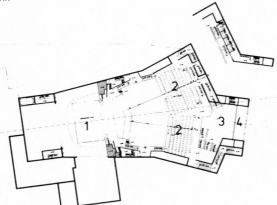

Plan at upper auditorium level;
1, stage; 2, upper tiers of seating;
3, inner foyer; 4, double window.

Auditorium. Photo credit:
Reinhard Friedrich.

which reads as much smaller than it is in fact.

The linear layout of the ground plan allows approach from both ends, leaving the hillside in front of the theatre as natural landscape. A service road comes up from behind the concert hall to allow access to the back of the stage, while the visitors' entrance with its approach road and car parking faces away from the town centre back towards the Porsche Strasse, shielded from view by trees. The end of the foyer is also connected by a direct path to a footbridge over

The building is divided into three parts: a central almost windowless mass contains stage, auditorium and flytower while two delicate wings extend outwards from it in opposite directions, one containing offices, dressing-rooms and caretaker's flat, the other forming an extensive foyer. The scaleless mass of the central part stands out on its hillside assertively, producing a similar kind of effect in its relationship with the townscape as some medieval castles do. Sheer bulk unbroken by elements at the human scale is in danger of seeming monumental and oppressive. However, the wings of the Wolfsburg theatre are deliberately set at the human scale and the single-storey foyer forms a buffer between the entrance and the bulk of the building, the length of the foyer making the auditorium appear quite small from the main entrance. This effect is cleverly heightened by the deliberately overscaled window at the back of the auditorium,

the Porsche Strasse, forming an easy pedestrian link with the town centre. The whole plan comes together as one of those flawlessly logical happy coincidences which recur in Scharoun's work, but we can be sure that it was only discovered as the result of a long and careful search.

As already mentioned the stage at Wolfsburg had to be conventional in size and shape to take readymade scenery, so it has the normal breadth to depth ratio of 39×26 ft. The auditorium, seating 750, appears on the ground-plan fairly conventional, too, with a symmetrical seating layout. Balcony seating is asymmetrical but it still appears in plan to be quite orderly. However, it is irregular in section as well as in plan since the balcony floor is not horizontal but slopes in both planes. The roof too is somewhat irregular and so is

the back end of the auditorium where it joins the foyer. This effect is heightened by the introduction of a huge window to throw daylight onto the stage, a feature borrowed from the earlier Kassel scheme. As a result of all these irregularities the space produced is complex and elusive. No doubt Scharoun was intending to disorientate his audience, as in the Mannheim project, by producing an 'aperspective' effect.

Top
Principal elevation, looking away from the town with trees as a backdrop.
Left
View to the left of the main entrance.
Right
View to the right of the main entrance.

Left and p34 above
Auditorium. Photos credit:
Reinhard Friedrich.

[33]

The foyer section of the building is as long as the rest put together but Scharoun has built it up very convincingly as a series of interlinked functions. There is a careful division of direct circulation from cloakroom circulation, defined by that characteristic Scharoun element, the small level-change with built-in seating. Also, part of the foyer designed to work as a restaurant is deliberately opened up with a large window and raised roof, facing downhill towards the town centre. Although this part of the space is not physically wider than the rest the window gives a degree of spatial continuity with the outside which makes it appear wider and, in consequence, it feels more static in character and less transient than the rest.

At Wolfsburg some of Scharoun's ideas about theatre design have finally been realised and the

theatre's success makes sadder still the missed opportunity at Kassel. Unfortunately Scharoun never saw the building in its finished state for he died just a year before its completion. It is a stunningly original conception, and despite the fact that he was seventy-two when he designed it, it contains no signs of tiredness or senility – in fact it shows a perfection of judgement perhaps exceeding that of his earlier work. It must rank among his greatest works, perhaps second only to the Philharmonie, and it is surely the best example in all his work of response to a site. That none of his competitors produced a remotely similar scheme is scarcely surprising, for even given the basic idea it is difficult to imagine who else could have carried it out convincingly. Who but Scharoun, for instance, could have handled that immensely long foyer with such decisive confidence, and who but he could have manipulated those irregular masses so successfully? The building forms a part of the landscape rather than standing aloof from it, and it was originally intended to dissolve into the hillside even more, as in the competition scheme Scharoun showed the foyer half buried in the hillside, its roof being continuous with the ground behind. One is reminded of Wright's statement that 'the land is the simplest form of architecture'. Scharoun's theatre can be seen as a careful manipulation of the landscape; the

way it becomes an inevitable part of its surroundings demonstrates very clearly how it was conceived as a place rather than as an imposed object, growing out of the requirements of the locality in an organic manner.

Above and p34 below
Wolfsburg theatre, 1965–73
Inner foyer. Photos credit:
Reinhard Friedrich.

Main foyer. Photo credit:
Reinhard Friedrich.

Chapter 3: The Concert Halls

Opposite top left
Philharmonie, Berlin, 1956–63.
Ground plan; 1, public entrances;
2, box office; 3, coat hanging for
left side of hall; 4, stairs to left
side of hall; 5, stairs to right side
of hall; 6, refreshments; 7, artists'
entrance; 8, offices; 9, goods
entrance; 10, caretaker's flat.
Opposite top right
Upper foyer plan (4–6 metres);
1, stairs to right side of hall;
2, coat hanging for right side of
hall; 3, stairs to left side of hall;
4, podium; 5, entrance to front
seats; 6, rehearsal room (entered
from intermediate landing).

Right
Exterior of hall as seen from
courtyard.

Site plan; 1, Tiergarten;
2, Philharmonie; 3, future
chamber music hall; 4, site of
future museums; 5, Church of St
Mathew; 6, future cultural hostel;
7, National Gallery by Mies van
der Rohe; 8, State Library by
Scharoun (under construction);
9, ring road; 10, canal.

Scharoun's concert hall designs are similar in many ways to his theatre designs. He considered both building types to have much the same kind of social significance, so he gave both about the same degree of architectural prominence. In both one finds the same basic design strategy: the auditorium is based on internal functions, being planned from the inside outwards, but it is surrounded by articulated ancillary parts which are positioned in response to siting and orientation, so the overall layout is planned from the outside inwards. The foyer then becomes the flexible element which reconciles these inward and outward forces.

In his most revolutionary theatre auditorium design, that of the Mannheim project described in the previous chapter, Scharoun advocated a very wide stage with a relatively shallow auditorium. One of his many reasons for doing this was that he wished to break down the barrier between actors and audience. Another was that he wished to even out as much as possible the quality of the seating, to eradicate as far as possible the distinction between good and bad seats – a distinction which would suggest to him social inequality. In his concert halls these two considerations become even more pronounced and one could go so far as to call the Philharmonic the first socialist concert hall. Scharoun describes his intentions in designing it as follows:

Music as the focal point: this was the keynote from the very beginning. This dominating thought not only gave shape to the auditorium of Berlin's new Philharmonie Hall but also ensured its undisputed priority within the entire building scheme. The orchestra and conductor stand spatially and optically in the very middle and if this is not the mathematical centre, nonetheless they are completely enveloped by their audience. Here you will find no segregation of 'producers' and 'consumers' but rather a community of listeners grouped around an orchestra in the most natural of all seating arrangements. Thus, despite its size, the auditorium has retained a certain intimacy, enabling a direct and co-creative share in the production of music. Here the creation and the experience of music occur in a hall not motivated by formal aesthetics, but whose design was inspired by the very purpose it serves. Man, music and space – here they meet in a new relationship.

The construction follows the pattern of a landscape, with the auditorium seen as a valley, and there at its bottom is the orchestra surrounded by a sprawling vineyard climbing the sides of its neighbouring hills. The ceiling, resembling a tent, encounters this 'landscape' like a 'skyscape'. Convex in character, the tent-like ceiling is very much linked with the acoustics, with the desire to obtain the maximum diffusion of music via the convex surfaces. Here the sound is not reflected from the narrow side of a hall, but rises from the depth and centre, moving towards all sides, descending and spreading evenly among the listeners below. Every effort was taken to transmit the sound waves to the most distant part of the auditorium by the shortest possible route. The diffusion is also served by the refraction of the auditorium walls, and the multi levelled, heterogeneous arrangement of the 'vineyard terraces'. In all this we were greatly aided by the progress made in the field of acoustic science. Here virgin territory has been discovered, explored and conquered.

The demands of the auditorium determine every last constructional detail of this monumental building. Even as far as the exterior form is concerned, a fact so clearly demonstrated by the tent-like shape of the roof. The construction

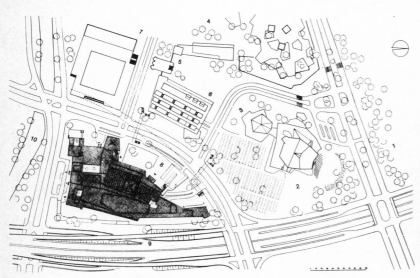

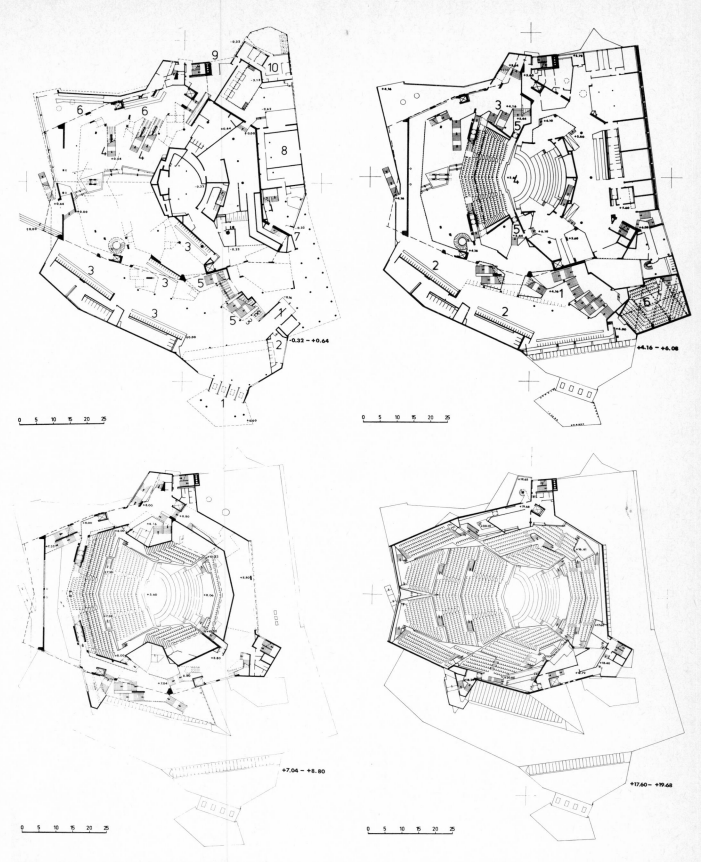

of the auditorium – built as it is over the main foyer – also determined the character of the ancillary space. Every room had ample opportunity for the free development of its own particular function. Even the complex of stairways seems to play about the foyer, yet rhythmically adapting its lively form to the demands of the auditorium.

Thus all is directed towards the preparation of the musical experience. The ancillary space stands in a dynamic and tense relationship to the festive calm of the auditorium, which is truly the jewel in the Philharmonic crown.[5]

Scharoun's expressive description of his hall in terms

of valley and tent is in a way misleading for it suggests a much more fanciful and less hard-headed approach than in fact was the case. The shape of the hall is certainly unorthodox and might at first sight seem arbitrary or sculptural in intention, especially to an architect conditioned to think in right angles. But in fact it is strictly functional and works better than most of its rectangular cousins in many ways, and within the terms of the values it represents it would be very hard to beat.

Bottom left
Plan at 7–9 metres.

Bottom right
Plan at 18–20 metres, showing auditorium in full.

[37]

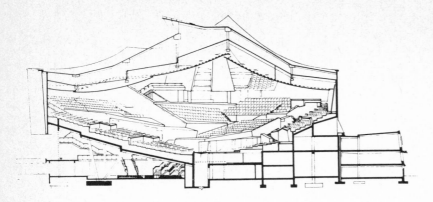

In a conventional hall a single mass of listeners sit facing the orchestra, passively outnumbering it. The space is essentially linear and the back seats are a very long way from the orchestra. In the Philharmonie the audience surround the orchestra, taking advantage of the fact that it radiates sound in all directions, and this results in a much more compact layout and a more enclosed, unified space. Thus although the hall seats over 2200 it is only 60 metres in length and the furthest seats from the podium are only 32 metres away: the distinction between good seats and bad seats has been reduced as much as possible. The seating is divided up into 'terraces', each accommodating about 300 people, breaking up the mass of the audience into units comparable in size with the orchestra. This also gives rise to a convenient circulation strategy in which each terrace has its own separate exit to the foyer at its own level. The steep banking of the sides of the hall allows the exit of lower terraces to be accommodated under upper terraces, reducing circulation space in plan to a minimum. The bowl-shaped section spreads the audience out vertically, again taking advantage of the omnidirectional sound radiation of the orchestra and giving each listener both a clear view of it and an un-

Interior of hall, two views.

broken sound path from it.

The unified musical event which Scharoun was trying to accommodate suggests perhaps a completely 'in the round' space with equally distributed seating on all sides, a sort of enlarged chapter house. However, this would be a negation of the axial layout of a traditional orchestra. On the other hand a completely linear layout is less compact and, although it is generally considered better to sit in front of an orchestra than behind or beside it, many people would prefer to sit near the orchestra and behind it (with the added advantage of facing the conductor) rather than in front and a long way off. The plan of the Philharmonie is effectively 'in the round' with a frontal bias, a careful compromise between the two extremes. Both the circular and the rectangular plan have bad acoustic properties, the former because its concave surfaces bring reflected sound to a focus rather than dispersing it, the latter because parallel surfaces promote standing waves and what is termed 'flutter echo'. In fact all simple geometrical plan shapes tend to generate acoustic problems because regular and repetitive forms can be frequency selective in their reflective properties and give rise to pronounced resonances. In the Philharmonie plan parallel walls have been carefully avoided. The small end of the hall is inverted for acoustic reasons: had it been flat it would have acted as a direct reflector down the axis causing an echo, and had it been pushed outwards rather than inwards a large concavity would have been created with an undesirable central focus. The other end of the hall where it becomes asymmetrical is also angled rather than being placed perpendicular to the axis, again to avoid directly axial reflections.

In section the two halves of the 'tent' roof are both convex and therefore disperse reflected sound very effectively. The space between them, which is in danger of acting as a concavity and producing an undesirable focus, is prevented from doing so by means of hanging reflectors which break the sound path and transmit some of the upward sound directly back to the audience nearby. Apart from the general shape the details of the hall interior are also irregular and each terrace of seating slopes in both planes at once, so hardly any surfaces are horizontal or vertical. Thus acoustic reflections off the terraces and terrace fronts tend to be randomly dispersed. As a result of all these measures, the hall has excellent acoustic properties. The reverberation time of the hall when occupied is a full two seconds. A commendable clarity of sound has been achieved without deadness; that dry lifeless quality which characterises some of the less successful modern concert halls has been completely avoided.

Orchestral performances in the Philharmonie sound rich, warm and natural without any loss of detail; the music seems to fill the hall and arrive from all directions.

As a visual experience the hall is quite remarkable and photographs give little idea of the strange quality of its shifting planes. The lack of normal perspective cues make accurate perception of the shape and size of the space very difficult. After sitting in one place for a while, one feels that one has grasped it, but then one only has to move slightly to be proved quite wrong. Walking around the hall and watching it change its apparent size is a fascinating experience. Just as in a real landscape hills appear much smaller from the middle of a valley than they do when one is standing on them, so the hall seems much smaller when seen from the centre than it does when seen from the edges. Most photographs one sees of it are taken from the edges with wide-angle lenses to get as much in as possible, showing the hall at its largest. From the centre the whole space seems much more intimate. The perceptual elusiveness of the hall can give us some idea of the kind of effect Scharoun was aiming for in his Mannheim theatre project and it would probably have been very effective.

The foyer of the Philharmonie runs around and underneath the hall linking up all the various terrace exits at different levels with a profusion of stairs and landings. The resultant space is so complex and labyrinthine that it is impossible to visualise as a unity and difficult to follow on plan. In practice it is not as disorientating as one might expect because circulation is skilfully controlled and one is always encouraged to move in the correct direction. Even when visiting the

Foyer. Photo credit: Reinhard Friedrich.

Philharmonie, Berlin, 1956–63
The labyrinthine foyer.

hall for the first time it is not difficult to find one's seat: all the levels are marked and their progression is obvious; one has only to ascend the complex of stairs and landings until one reaches the appropriate level. The fluidity of the circulation results largely from the use of the kind of devices we saw in the Kassel foyer. Stairs are angled so that one arrives at a landing facing the direction in which one is next intended to go, direction changes being made at landings where they can be controlled without ambiguity. All circulation elements are carefully sized and after a concert one can watch the crowd flowing out of the hall with surprising rapidity and without congestion. As the various routes join up they become larger in much the same way as a river enlarges as more and more tributaries flow into it. As with most of Scharoun's foyers, that of the Philharmonie is formally subservient to the hall and was conceived as a link between the various hall terraces

Right. Photo credit: Reinhard Friedrich.

and the main entrance, including cloakroom facilities on the way. The totally broken-up space of the foyer provides a dramatic foil to the unified space of the hall and conjures up a sense of excitement and expectation appropriate to a festive occasion.

Scharoun was commissioned to build the Philharmonie as a result of winning a competition held in '56. The site chosen for the competition was not that on which the building now stands; it was an open space off Bundesallee not far from Kurfürstendamm, the new centre of West Berlin. The concert hall was to have been built onto the back of a neo-classical school with a massive colonnaded entrance which was to have served the concert hall as well, and to have linked it with the street. Scharoun's competition entry had a hall little different from that eventually built, except that it had a few large exits rather than a separate one for each terrace. The foyer was designed as a link between the hall and the entrance colonnade of the old school and is reminiscent of the foyer in the Kassel project which linked theatre and road bridge. However, whereas the Kassel foyer splits in plan to serve the two sides of the auditorium separately, that of the Philharmonie does so in section. Just beyond the colonnade a prominent range of steps were planned to take visitors with tickets for the right-hand side of the hall to cloakroom facilities on the first floor, while those with tickets for the left-hand side would use cloakroom facilities on the ground floor planned in the same way.

After the competition had taken place the site was changed and the building was constructed at a corner of the Tiergarten in central Berlin a few hundred yards from the notorious wall. Other cultural buildings are being built there too, with the intention that when the wall is finally demolished and Berlin is re-united this cultural zone will stand in the centre of the city. Scharoun adapted his design to the new site rather than starting again from scratch. He retained both the non-axial main entrance and the two-level cloakroom arrangement. This proved convenient as, by keeping the foyer predominantly to one side of the hall, he was able to leave the other side accessible to musicians, administrators and technicians without any difficulty. Apart from the hall and foyer the building contains numerous ancillary parts which have been allowed to grow out of it as required in a rather informal manner. The growth process is not complete, since a chamber music hall, a museum of musical instruments and an

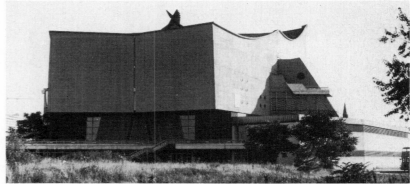

institute for musical research have been planned by Scharoun and will be added to the hall.

This organic planning policy results in a complex, fragmented external form which has been allowed to happen in response to internal requirements, a form discovered in the planning process rather than imposed as a preconception. As one walks around the building the various parts shift in relation to each other and the overall form remains elusive in much the same way as that of the internal spaces does – it has a complexity that makes it somehow ungraspable. As a landmark the Philharmonie works well and has taken a prominent role in Berlin life beyond its function as a concert hall. Berliners have a curious affection for it, they nearly all love the hall itself but many have reservations about the exterior, finding it ugly. However, it has such a strong personality that discussion of whether it is beautiful or ugly becomes in a way irrelevant. Once one understands how the form was generated it seems inevitable because its visual image quality is so closely linked with its whole raison d'être.

Top. Philharmonie, Berlin, 1956–63.
View from west. Photo credit: Reinhard Friedrich.
Centre. From east.
Bottom. From north.

[41]

Unfortunately the site on which the Philharmonie stands is flat and open, whereas the original competition site was more distinctly urban and enclosed with buildings. In my opinion the exterior is more effective and appealing seen from close to than from far off, and it would probably relate better to a site in which it was at least partially enclosed by other buildings than it does to its present site. The main reason for this is the compactness of the layout. Had Scharoun started with the present site he would probably have produced a more spread out building, perhaps more like the Kassel theatre project. He might have put his hall on the ground and wound the foyer around rather than underneath it, which would have resulted in a building with a gentler external profile.

At present the Philharmonie is in a kind of wilderness between roads, though other cultural buildings are being built around it which should improve the situation. Mies' National Gallery is already there and the massive state library by Scharoun is half completed. A museum is being planned and the aforementioned chamber music hall and museum of musical instruments should eventually be built as well. The feeling that the Philharmonie stands in a wilderness is greatly exaggerated by an almost total lack of external maintenance. The external surfaces of the building were originally intended to be covered in insulation and a copper outer skin to protect the concrete against Berlin's severe winter temperatures. However, at the time when it was built there was not enough

money to provide this external skin despite the fact that the building was relatively cheap and the bare concrete was painted in white and ochre, the ochre being chosen by Scharoun as reminiscent of old Prussian palaces. Since then the paint has not been renewed and is now flaking off in places, and the concrete has cracked. There are plans now to insulate the building by covering the outside in translucent polyester sheeting with a golden metallic underside. What it will look like then is hard to imagine!

The landscaping around the Philharmonie has also suffered from neglect. Hermann Mattern's original layout included a garden for use in the interval but now the area is covered in scrub and coarse grass. The addition of a few trees would effect a considerable improvement. When the cultural zone which includes the Philharmonie is complete and the building and its surrounding landscape are maintained as they should be we shall be able to judge better just how successful as a monument the Philharmonie can be. It is a pity that it has been kept so badly as it is certainly Scharoun's best known building, and is widely considered to be his masterpiece.

The competition for the Philharmonie took place in '56 and the building was completed in '63. During this period Scharoun also worked on another concert hall design, an entry for the Saarbrücken competition of '58 which was awarded third prize. Although this project was conceived at the same time as the revised version of the Philharmonie it was not a variation on the

Saarbrücken, Concert Hall project, 1958

Upper foyer plan (*left*) and hall plan.

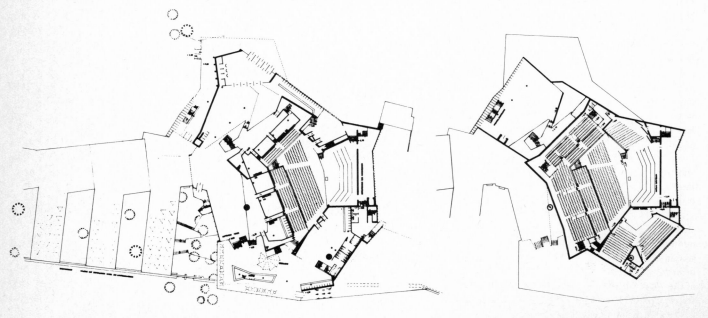

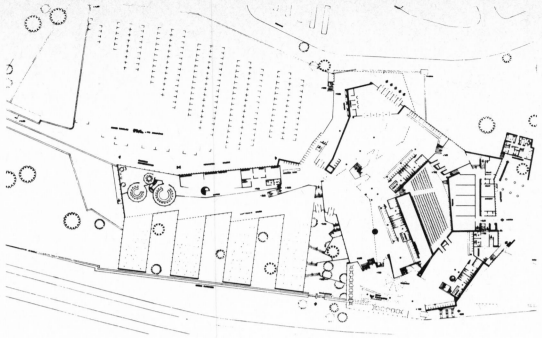

Section and elevation.

same theme as one might have expected but grew in a different way in response to different requirements. The project contained a large and a small hall which could be used together or separately, being divided by movable partitions. The large hall was smaller than that of the Philharmonie and was required for occasional film shows and lectures as well as concerts. Thus the 'in the round' layout was rejected in favour of a more conventional juxtaposition of audience and orchestra, but in a way the hall is more irregular than the Philharmonie for it is completely asymmetrical, the seating layout being broken up in a manner reminiscent of the Mannheim theatre project. A characteristically loose foyer winds around the hall, linking it up with a completely non-axial entrance and an exhibition gallery which extends the building westwards.

After the success of the Philharmonie and the acclaim that followed its opening one might have expected Scharoun to repeat his design, at least in its basic principles, in his next concert hall scheme, but instead he moved in quite a different direction. The Pforzheim competition took place in '64 and has never been published. Scharoun's entry did not gain any award. As in the Saarbrücken project large and small halls can be used separately or together but the large hall has an implied symmetry. It gains its form from the curved back wall which was designed to act as a parabolic reflector for the orchestra, and though seating is 'in the round' only a very small proportion of it is actually behind the orchestra. As usual the ancillary parts of the complex, which include a restaurant and conference hall, are separately articulated and the foyer is somewhat irregular. However, the staircases and main entrance are surprisingly formal and recti-linear like those of the Zurich theatre scheme conceived in the same year.

Scharoun's last concert hall, yet to be built, is the chamber music hall which will be added to the Philharmonie. The main hall was constructed with this extension in mind, its approximate size and position having been decided quite early on, but the detailed design of the chamber hall dates from the mid-sixties and is stylistically closer to the Pforzheim hall and Zurich

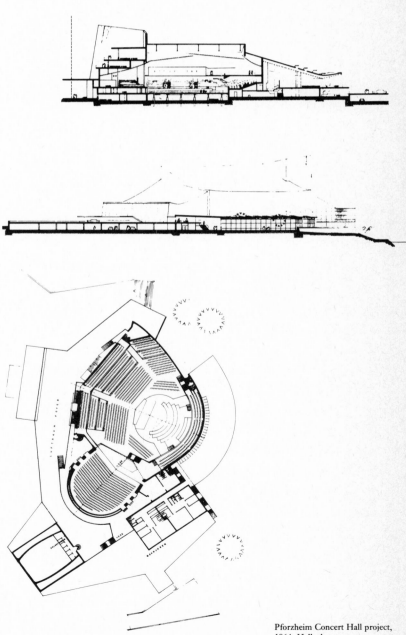

[43]

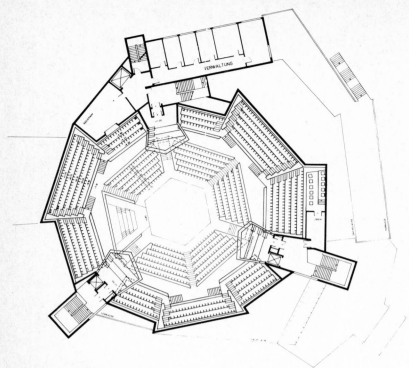

Chamber Music Hall for the
Philharmonie, 1972.
Hall plan.

Ground floor plan (see p36 for
site plan).

theatre than to the Philharmonie. The layout of the chamber hall is completely 'in the round,' growing outwards from a central hexagonal podium. The hexagonal geometry allows a convenient structural arrangement and a triaxial entry and staircase system. But as always with Scharoun the discipline is rejected when it ceases to be useful, and the outer parts of the hall break into a more complex geometry to escape the acoustic disadvantages of such a regular form as the hexagon. Thus parallel surfaces are avoided and sound path distances between the centre and the outer walls are varied. The hall will probably be constructed in the late seventies and will seat approximately 1000 people.

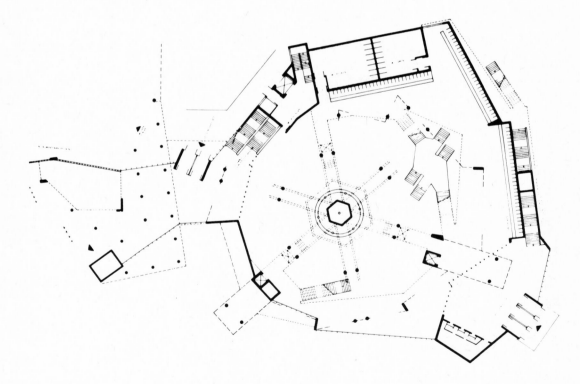

Chapter 4: Housing

Prototype family house at the Weissenhof exhibition, Stuttgart, 1927.

Scharoun was a committed socialist* and he devoted much of his energy to housing problems throughout his career. In '27 he designed a prototype family house for the Weissenhof exhibition in Stuttgart, which is generally considered his first mature built work, and between '27 and '33, when the Nazis came to power and outlawed modern architecture, he produced a steady stream of designs for apartment buildings and prototypes for cheap one-family houses, some prefabricated. A Berlin exhibition for which Scharoun designed a prototype house bore the title Sun, Air and Houses for All, which epitomises the spirit of the period.

Perhaps the most famous of all Scharoun's projects done before the war was Siemensstadt, a *Sozialer Wohnungsbau*, a housing development for low-income groups, built for the Siemens electrical workers on the outskirts of Berlin. Scharoun was responsible for the overall layout of this large scheme which was made up of several groups of apartment blocks by different

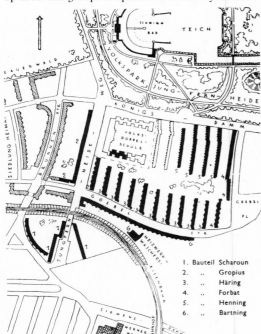

1. Bauteil	Scharoun
2. ,,	Gropius
3. ,,	Häring
4. ,,	Forbat
5. ,,	Henning
6. ,,	Bartning

architects. He also designed some of the most interesting and individual blocks with revolutionary flat plans. Seeking a new focus for the dwelling now that the hearth had been superseded by central heating he

evolved the idea of the 'room in the middle', a large living/dining space which took up the full depth of the building having windows on both façades. Space which could only be used for circulation was eliminated as far as possible. Although Siemensstadt was

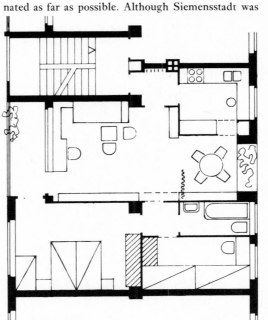

Siemensstadt, Berlin, 1930. Plan of a typical flat in one of Scharoun's blocks.

Left. Siemensstadt, Berlin, 1930. Site plan.

essentially low-cost housing it still seems remarkably generous today. It amply demonstrates that the blocks in a park idea can work quite well provided that the vegetation is allowed to mature. Scharoun himself lived in one of his flats in Siemensstadt until 1960 when he moved to one of the studio flats in the neighbouring development, North-Charlottenburg, the postwar extension of Siemensstadt which he planned in '56 and built between '56 and '61.

The brief for North-Charlottenburg was much the same as that for Siemensstadt, another *Sozialer Wohnungsbau* with a similar density, and a comparison of the two schemes is therefore quite relevant. The Siemensstadt apartment blocks were youthful works full of the vigour and uncompromising determination characteristic of the early modern movement. At the time 'white architecture' must have seemed quite shocking, and its image quality was unashamedly Utopian. Now the Siemensstadt seems very much a period piece tinged with nostalgia, especially with its very off-white render cracking in places and falling off.

* Scharoun was socialist in the broad sense of being very committed to the solution of social problems and trying to provide a high standard of accommodation for all, rather than in the directly political sense; he was not affiliated to any political party.

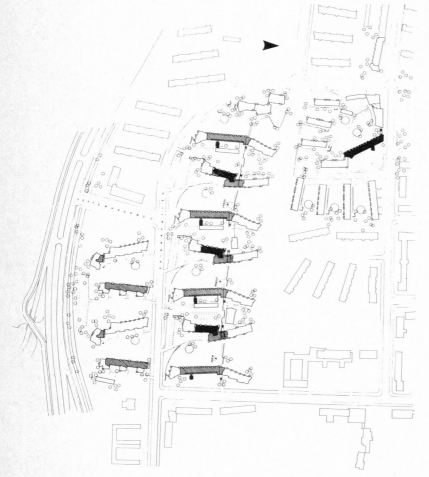

The North-Charlottenburg apartment blocks have raised less enthusiasm among critics than those that Scharoun built in the thirties, perhaps because they are less striking visually, though they are more complex in plan and offer more to their inhabitants. The essential difference is one of image quality. After the war things had changed considerably, a second generation of architects in the modern style had demonstrated how banal its application could be, and the Utopian image was irrevocably tarnished. Scharoun had been forced to build in traditional materials throughout the Nazi period and this drew him away from the 'white architecture' for good. Besides, as his experience grew so did his ability to extract some formal identity for a building out of the programme. Conscious styling became less and less important, the basic concept of a scheme being always his primary concern. North-Charlottenburg has an unsurprising everyday quality because it is a housing scheme. Unlike so many other architects of the modern movement Scharoun successfully resisted the temptation to build a monument for every project, instead he sought a scale and an imagery appropriate to each situation. The

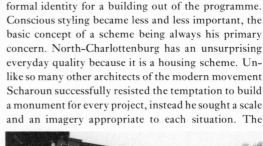

image quality of North-Charlottenburg is the inevitable result of the way it was planned and, though there are playful touches here and there which can be regarded as styling, these are not of fundamental importance and nowhere do they challenge the basic concept.

It must be fairly clear from earlier chapters how Scharoun attempted to derive form from function – to give substance to the 'essence' of a brief. We have seen how, in his schools particularly, he articulated the parts of a building to produce a form that reflected its social contents. Applying this idea to housing one would expect to find the house or flat as the fundamental unit setting the scale of the whole complex, as it reflects the family which is the fundamental social unit. But what of the differentiation between the units? No two families are exactly the same so perhaps no two flats should be the same either. How can the theory of organic building respond to this suggestion? In a real 'organic' situation such as an unplanned medieval town, a model to which Scharoun often referred, houses were built one by one according to the needs and wishes of their owners, and thus each owner expressed himself in his building and each building differed from the next. However, this variety was contained within a discipline of construction which produced a consistency of building type and differentiation between different building types. A townscape of great richness grew which was fully expressive of its original occupants without losing its overall coherence.

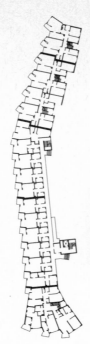

Modern mass housing is in contrast very banal and repetitive because it is produced by a much simpler process, each scheme being conceived by one or at best only a few minds, and being harshly limited by economic construction and building regulations. The bland monotony of such developments is widely resented and architects have failed to convince the public that it is either necessary or desirable. Lining people up in straight rows of identical dwellings is like forcing them to wear a uniform; it is repressive. Ideally, perhaps, we could avoid uniformity by repeating the generative process of a medieval town, planning each building or apartment in response to the particular needs and tastes of its future occupants. But such a policy is hardly practicable in the present situation. All that we can do in practice is to introduce as much variety of room type, flat type, block type and general layout as possible within economic and technical limitations. Then, even if an inhabitant of a flat has no say in its design, he can at least identify with his particular unit and see that it is different from the next one.

At North-Charlottenburg Scharoun introduced a degree of variety unusual in low-cost mass housing. Like parts of Siemensstadt it consists essentially of slab blocks aligned north to south so that the sun can penetrate into the spaces between them. The blocks vary in height between three storeys and twelve, the largest being placed at the centre of the site. They are for the most part one dwelling thick, so nearly all the flats have

more than one outlook, but at the southern ends of the blocks the linear arrangement gives way to a series of angled flats fanned out to take advantage of the sunlight and view. Access is provided either through staircases, each serving a pair of dwellings per floor, or in the higher parts by means of access galleries served by common lifts. The larger blocks, which vary in height, contain a mixture of stair and gallery access. The external forms of the blocks are somewhat irregular in response to the way in which the flats were put together for the flat plans were the starting-point, the blocks taking their forms from the flats rather than vice versa. This policy has the advantage that each flat type can grow to its natural shape without too much compromise, allowing well proportioned rooms and an economical distribution of space. So often when flats are forced into a rigid shell or made to answer to a modular grid they seem cramped and awkward, with spaces that feel pinched or mean. Scharoun's flats have in contrast an air of ease and freedom that seems deceptively casual. Where he departs from the rectangle in his plans he always makes good use of the irregularities thus induced, and if one tries to straighten out these irregularities and make them rectangular they just will not go, the angles are inherent in the layout, not just stylistic quirks. Scharoun exploited various possibilities of different positions and orientations to produce a range of different flats each having particular advantages and disadvantages.

A block on the south side of the development.

Top left
Typical floor plans of six–nine storey blocks

Left
Typical flat plans on the south end of a block.

A garden between blocks in the centre of the development.

North-Charlottenburg development, Berlin, 1956–61 One of the meandering, informal paths.

The north to south alignment of the blocks is only approximate since they are never entirely straight or parallel-sided. The largest are cranked centrally to produce a series of alternating spaces between them. Each space bounded by the two concave façades contains a service road and parking at one end and a recessed lawn at the other. These lawns feel much more enclosed and protected than those which make up the spaces between the convex façades. The latter seem much more open and promote a greater feeling of continuity with spaces to the north and south of the blocks, and they also get more sunlight because of the diverging buildings. The differentiation of open spaces is taken further by some very effective landscaping and now that the trees are maturing there is a variety of green spaces of different shapes and sizes, including bushy paths between trees, quiet shady spots where elderly people sit in summer and unpretentious children's playgrounds which are well used. The development has an atmosphere that is quiet, pleasant and humane. Irregular placing of the buildings makes it seem very casual in comparison with the sort of rectilinear housing schemes that we see so much of these days. This quality does not really come out in photographs because perspective depends on parallel lines and if they are not present one gets an inaccurate impression of space. In fact photographs make it look rather ordinary, particularly black and white photographs which omit its varied colour scheme. In some ways it is ordinary: there are no flashy self-conscious details, no great aesthetic statement, nothing proclaiming 'this is Great Architecture'. But on the other hand it is unusual because of the responsiveness and sensitivity of its planning and the lack of imposed aesthetic discipline, which may make it anathema to some but which I find humble and accommodating.

North-Charlottenburg owes a certain amount to an earlier scheme with a much more dramatic image, the Romeo and Juliet flats at Stuttgart-Zuffenhausen built between '54 and '59 in collaboration with Wilhelm Frank. This project was effectively the prototype for all Scharoun's later medium and high rise housing projects. It is considerably smaller than North-Charlottenburg and was a private development, containing shops and restaurant as well as flats. The site, part of a hillside just outside old Zuffenhausen, is roughly triangular in shape and lies next to a busy road junction. Scharoun decided to build two blocks offering more or less equal amounts of accommodation: the one at the narrow end of the site would have to be tall and thin, while that at the wide end could be short and fat. This arrangement would assure that the main vertical accent of the development fell next to the road junction, the busiest part, and would allow the upper levels of the tall block, already uphill of the other, to see over it.

In any block of flats over four storeys high lifts are usually considered a necessity and, being expensive, they must be shared between as many flats as possible. This inevitably means that a high block has one main vertical axis with lifts and horizontal means of access on each floor. This access can either take the form of a central corridor with flats on both sides, an economical arrangement but one that results in dreary corridors devoid of daylight and flats with only one outlook, or it can take the form of side access galleries usually exposed to the weather like those at North-Charlottenburg. Scharoun always chose the latter alternative in a building of any length, but was willing to choose the former for a building of compact

Romeo and Juliet, Stuttgart-Zuffenhausen, 1954–9. Site plan and aerial photograph.

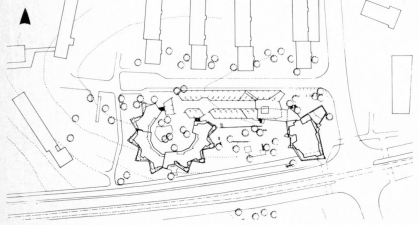

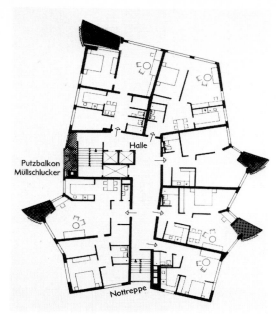

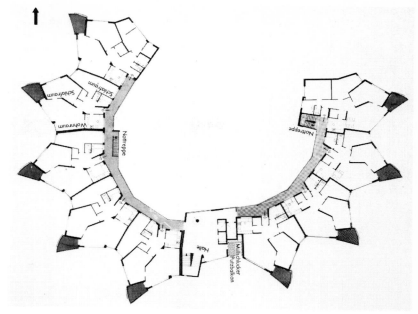

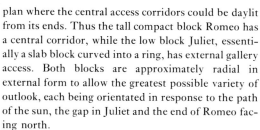

plan where the central access corridors could be daylit from its ends. Thus the tall compact block Romeo has a central corridor, while the low block Juliet, essentially a slab block curved into a ring, has external gallery access. Both blocks are approximately radial in external form to allow the greatest possible variety of outlook, each being orientated in response to the path of the sun, the gap in Juliet and the end of Romeo facing north.

As at North-Charlottenburg individual flats are externally recognisable by their balconies and window patterns as well as by changes in angle of façade, but in Juliet this differentiation is taken further as each vertical set of flats is painted in a different colour. However, despite the fact that the flats are articulated the block remains a very strong statement in itself, and in the eyes of the world it is to a block that a family belong rather than to a flat. Scharoun therefore tried wherever possible to give his blocks definite separate identities. The difference between Romeo and Juliet had been at first a response to the site, but he went on to develop it, creating a subtle counterpoint between them. Romeo commands his corner of the site in a way that is hard and perhaps a little uninviting. He is rather repetitive in section, which tends to conceal the variety in his plan. Juliet is in contrast much softer, standing at the green end of the site and whirling around with her penthouse flats tumbling from twelve to five storeys in a kind of irregular spiral. She is much more enchanting and inviting than Romeo, yet without his presence she would be much weaker.

Critics would be wrong to assume that because of the name *Romeo and Juliet*, Shakespeare's play was in any sense the inspiration of the scheme, or to assume that it was motivated by any conscious symbolism. Scharoun was determined to give it a name, but this came late in the project after it had been worked out in principle, if not in detail. He asked those in his office at the time to propose one and there were several fruitless discussions. One evening, as he was about to leave, he glanced again at the model and was struck by the male and female natures of the forms: 'Ah, Romeo and Juliet'. Romeo and Juliet it remained. At first its inhabitants were a little shy of the names but soon they became an established part of Stuttgart life. After all, 'I live in Romeo' is a great deal more memorable than 'I live in block 42B'.

Left
Romeo, typical floor plan.

Right
Juliet, typical floor plan.

Romeo, west side.

Below
Juliet, west side.

'Salute', Stuttgart-Fasanenhof,
1961–3.
View from south east.

Right
Typical upper floor plan.

Scharoun's greatest achievement in Romeo and
Juliet is his having created a strong sense of place where
none existed before, something very few modern
architects have managed to do. But at the same time
he created a housing scheme which has proved both
efficient and economic, with flats that are much sought
after. The difference between Romeo and Juliet and
its rectangular rivals is not simply a matter of style but
a difference in degree of visual and spatial richness.
Its complexity of form makes it a mine of visual excitement, while the contrast between the two blocks provides an endless formal dialogue. Unlike most modern
housing schemes its spaces cannot be seen and appreciated in five minutes. It provides, rather, a spatial experience which can evolve over a long period.

Romeo and Juliet proved commercially successful
and brought Scharoun some other housing commissions in the Stuttgart area. The first of these was a
single block of flats named Salute at Stuttgart-
Fasanenhof, which he designed again in collaboration with Wilhelm Frank. Here no two flats on the
same floor are alike, and a variety of flat sizes has
resulted in an unusually varied social spectrum of
occupants. In keeping with the idea that the block
represents to some extent a social unit the ground floor
contains community functions: a laundry, kinder-

garten and driving school. The roof, like those of
Romeo and Juliet, carries set-back studio flats at varied
levels. Salute is based on exactly the same principles
as Romeo and Juliet and has been constructed and
finished in much the same way, but the ground plan

Below right
Main entrance.

Ground floor plan.

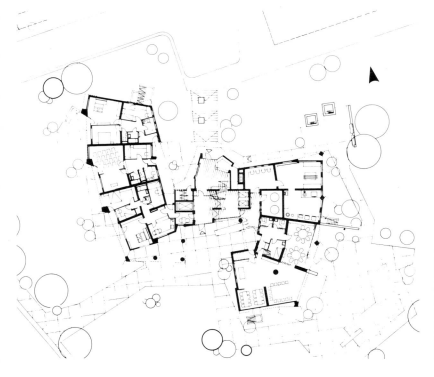

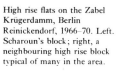

exploits a new and ingenious possibility. Similar in a way to Romeo, having approximately the same sort of radial layout, the two halves are split about the north to south axis and displaced to allow each flat a rear outlook while preserving an economical circulation layout. The larger flat plans are based on the idea of avoiding wastage of space on circulation through combining dining space and hall – two functions that will not conflict provided that the family eat together.

The ideas developed at Stuttgart later came to a surprising climax in Berlin. In '66 Scharoun designed a massive apartment block, on the same principles as Romeo and Juliet but much larger, which stands beside Zabel Krügerdamm not far from Märkisches Viertel. For some unaccountable reason it has not yet acquired a name.

The Germans seem much more conditioned to flat dwelling than we are, and there has been no strong reaction in Germany against high rise flats. In Berlin, not only are more and more being built but they seem to be getting larger and larger every year. The new Märkisches Viertel is awe-inspiring to say the least;

in terms of sheer scale it makes Roehampton look very tame. Scharoun's monster block, huge though it is, stands in a landscape full of developments of a similar scale and does not seem out of place, on the contrary it makes a refreshing contrast to its dull, monumental, rectangular rivals. Thus in actuality it seems less forceful than it appears in photographs. One would perhaps expect any tower block of this size to be quite overwhelming, but its fragmentation and the constant assertion of the human scale reduce its apparent bulk and its complexity is fascinating. The block has so

Views of the complex exterior.

High rise flats on the Zabel
Krügerdamm, Berlin
Reinickendorf, 1966–70. Typical
upper floor plan below.

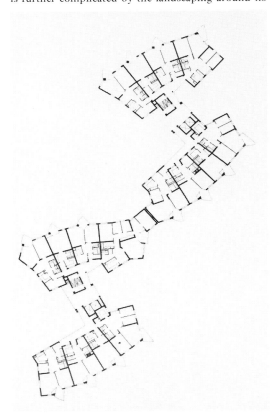

many sides at different angles that it is extremely difficult when walking around it on the ground to work
out what the shape of the plan might be. The issue
is further complicated by the landscaping around its

base. A path runs up an incline on one side which
appears to be part of the ground, but after passing
under the building between its columns one finds oneself on a footbridge, the natural ground level being that
of the road below. In fact the plan turns out to be a
fairly simple development of that of Salute, being
effectively two Salute blocks tied together, though the
variations in section and the landscaping around the
base make it appear more complicated.

The massiveness of the block is inevitable, but it is
not an oppressive massiveness because the building
has so much personality. It seems to stand as an assertion of individuality in what is otherwise becoming
rather a bland and depressing landscape. To me it
seemed like a monster, but a friendly monster. Photographs unfortunately remove much of its vitality by
flattening it, taking it out of context and losing its
varied colour scheme.

The last high rise block which Scharoun designed
stands at Böblingen near Stuttgart and is named
Orplid. It is a ring block similar in plan to Juliet, taking advantage of a sloping south facing site and was
completed in '73. Romeo and Juliet, Salute, Orplid
and the Zabel Krügerdamm block were all high rise
developments in areas given over to high rise. Characteristically Scharoun produced buildings of a scale
appropriate to their sites and had no general commitment to high rise solutions. In fact over the years
he produced housing schemes of almost every type.

Rauher Kapf is a new low density suburb of Böblingen, near Stuttgart. It was built on virgin countryside and is still surrounded by woods. The development was private and contains a mixture of detached

'Orplid', Böblingen, near
Stuttgart, 1969–71. Second floor
plan.

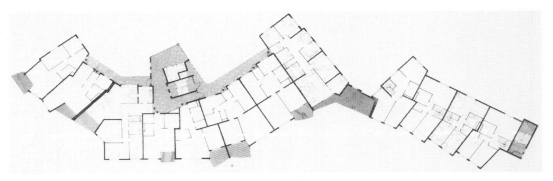

[52]

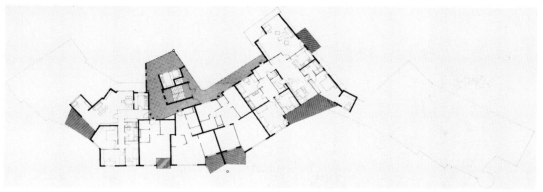

'Orplid', Böblingen, near Stuttgart, 1969–71. Tenth floor plan and model below.

houses, terraced houses and low rise flats. Scharoun was commissioned to design the centrepiece, a series of small blocks of flats set in a kind of garden. He produced two block types, one of four and one of six storeys, which are similar in plan to the southern ends of the blocks at North-Charlottenburg. In each block three large flats radiate from a single staircase, the back flats in each case being entered off one set of landings and the front flats off the other, a circulation arrangement which could scarcely be more economical. As usual the flats are fanned out to take advantage of the path of the sun, the north sides being relatively blank.

Above
Rauher Kapf housing development, Böblingen, near Stuttgart, 1965.

Above left
Typical floor plan of a six storey block.

Left
Typical floor plan of a four storey block.

Bottom left
West side of a six storey block.

Below
Site plan

Rauher Kapf housing development. West side of a four storey block.

Courtyard housing project, Heligoland, 1952. Diagrammatic ground floor plan.

All of the buildings are finished in pink or yellow render.

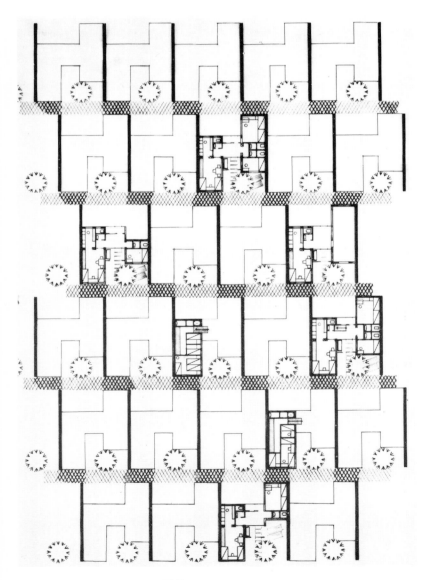

The blocks are set into the landscape in a fairly casual way to leave quite a large unobstructed garden in the centre. At one end of the site stands a two-storey building containing community facilities, food shop, launderette, hairdresser, youth club and caretaker's flat. Next to it seventy-five garages and a heating plant for the whole complex are hidden underground. The landscaping treatment is sensitive and unobtrusive; the ground undulates gently and enough vegetation has been provided in the form of small trees and shrubs to prevent it feeling bare despite the present lack of mature trees. Paths run to and fro just directly enough without seeming strict. A sort of focus is provided in the form of a little bridge over an artificial pond which might seem to some a little twee, but is convincingly done. A children's playground is provided behind the community building.

Rauher Kapf is at once the most subtle and least photographable of Scharoun's housing schemes. It is a masterpiece of understatement, in many ways rather plain, but nonetheless astonishingly gentle. The quiet wooded site helps of course but the gentleness comes mainly, I think, from the freedom with which the buildings are placed and from the total lack of aesthetically motivated rigidity. It remains my favourite Scharoun housing scheme.

Although most of Scharoun's housing output consisted of blocks of flats and of course private houses, he did in various projects turn to other forms when he thought them appropriate. In a prize-winning competition entry for a development in Heligoland of '52 he turned to a form of courtyard housing. He wanted to produce a small scale village-like atmosphere, and because of the island situation vehicles did not have to be accommodated. The courtyards are formed by pairs of houses rather than being private and the access alleyways run through them, sacrificing some privacy for the sake of community interaction. The dwelling itself is highly flexible and can be extended from the normal single-storey to two if required. Six different versions of it were indicated in the plan. The basic layout seems surprisingly rigid and repetitive for Scharoun; no doubt it was partly conditioned by the

[54]

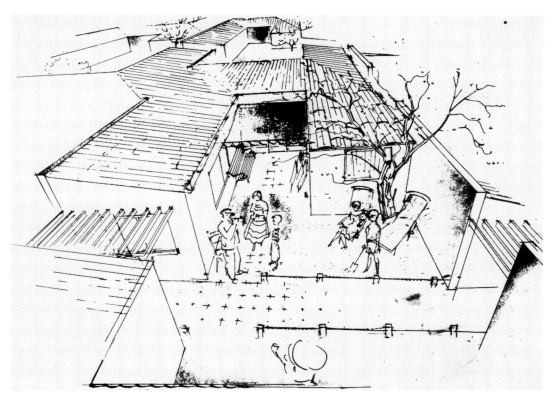

Courtyard housing project,
Heligoland, 1952.
Perspective sketch.

Project for an old people's home,
Tiergarten, Berlin, 1952. Ground
floor plan; 1, main entrance;
2, coats; 3, kitchen; 4, communal
hall; 5, stage; 6, table store when
hall used for lectures, films, etc.,
rather than dining; 7, staff dining-
room; 8, central hall; 9, ramp to
first floor; 10, shop and
newsagent; 11, bathrooms;
12, workshops and handicraft
rooms; 13, exit to garden; 14, two
persons' bed-sitting room wing;
15, day-room; 16, garden; 17, one
person's bed-sitting room wing.

construction required to achieve flexibility, and in any case the variations in dwelling type would add a considerable degree of interest.

Of a similar scale to the Heligoland scheme is another that Scharoun designed in the same year. This was a competition entry for an old people's home in Berlin. It is largely one-storey, consisting of rows of small flats strung out along corridors divided by strips of communal open space. The ends of the corridors run into a building containing grouped community facilities, including a dining-room, bathrooms, and a variety of leisure-rooms. The formal articulation is familiar and as one might expect the dwellings face approximately southward while the communal facilities run parallel to the street. In general layout it bears a surprising resemblance to the later Geschwister

Scholl school. This project was quite unlike the rest of the competition entries and the judges felt obliged to award Scharoun first prize because of its sheer brilliance. However they felt that he had been too liberal in his interpretation of the brief, and that the building was bound to be too expensive. It therefore remained unbuilt.

This cross-section of Scharoun's work has, I hope, served as an adequate introduction to his achievements and architectural philosophy. It must be called a cross-section rather than a summary because of the 215 projects listed in '69 only twenty have so far been discussed. Some major works are still to come, but those can be left until later in this book, for now we are familiar enough with Scharoun's ideas to investigate where they came from and how they developed. In the next part Scharoun's biographical and historical background will be investigated and the prewar works, which have so far received scant attention, will be given a more extensive coverage.

Project for one old people's home, Tiergarten, Berlin, 1952.

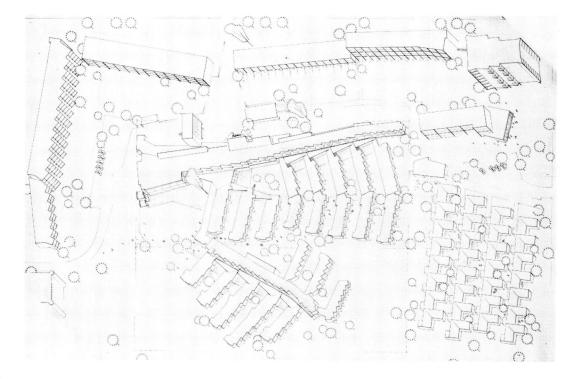

PART II
Chapter 5: The Early Years

The architects who brought about the modern movement in European architecture fall very largely into two generations. The early pioneers, who dominate the period between the turn of the century and the First World War, were mostly born in the 1860s: Hermann Muthesius 1861, Henri van de Velde '63, Peter Behrens '68, Tony Garnier and Hans Poelzig '69, Adolf Loos '70, Auguste Perret '74. The second generation, who finally established modern architecture as we know it, were born in the 1880s: Hugo Häring '82, Walter Gropius and Theo van Doesburg '83, Ludwig Mies van der Rohe '86, Le Corbusier and Erich Mendelsohn '87, Gerrit Rietveldt '88. Following the second generation, a few important figures were born in the 1890s and came to their maturity in the late 1920s: Hans Scharoun (b. '93) was one and Alvar Aalto (b. '98) another. They are the men who took part in the original struggle of the heroic period and yet were still building in the early seventies. History has not yet assimilated them.

Hans Scharoun was born in Bremen, a large city in northern Germany on the banks of the river Weser. His father's family were craftsmen, originally from Bohemia. His mother's family owned a smithy at Lüneberg. He had one older and one younger brother but large age gaps precluded a close relationship with either. While the boy was still very young the family moved to Bremerhaven where his father became the manager of a brewery. It was here that Scharoun spent the whole of his childhood and the atmosphere of the port made a lasting impression upon him.

Quite often architects seem to have a predisposition towards the kind of atmosphere they grew up in and they reproduce it in their work, not in an obvious and conscious manner but in a rather subtle and intangible way. Things familiar in early childhood take a prominent part in the development of consciousness and become deeply embedded in one's identity, tied perhaps to a conception of home. In Scharoun's case a childhood spent around a busy port resulted, it seems, in a permanent underlying affection for the marine world. Marine elements occur frequently in his work,

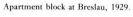

Apartment block at Breslau, 1929.

Project for a church at
Bremerhaven, 1911, perspective
sketch.

portholes, ventilation grills, steel handrails, and so do
ship-like forms. His most 'marine' building is the Breslau apartment block of 1929. Here we find not only
the clean white forms, portholes and handrails, but
also a structure inevitably reminiscent of a ship's
bridge, walls that step up and down with that quarter-
circle that one finds on ships, and frames like those
found on the decks of ships. Whether all this borrow-
ing was conscious or not remains unclear. Ocean liners
had been noticed as a kind of source for modern architecture earlier, Le Corbusier included a photograph
of one in *Vers une Architecture*, but nobody else's version of the International Style was quite as marine as
Scharoun's.

As a schoolboy Scharoun decided early on that he
wanted to become an architect and he spent much of
his spare time in drawing and sketching local architecture. At the age of fourteen he delivered a lecture
to his schoolfellows entitled Modern Architecture in
Bremerhaven. But his father, an unimaginative man
not receptive to his son's ideas, had a more financially
secure and respectable profession in mind. He
attempted to curb his son's natural inclinations by for-
bidding him to sketch but the boy continued on the
sly, aided and abetted by his mother. In 1911 his father

died and Scharoun had no difficulty in entering a
public architectural competition for a church in Bremerhaven. His scheme is not in itself particularly remarkable. It has obvious stylistic leanings towards Art
Nouveau architecture, of which there are a few good
examples in Bremerhaven, but it seems remarkably
competent when considered as the work of a seven-
teen-year-old.

In 1912 Scharoun took up architectural studies in
Berlin at the Technical Highschool, Charlottenburg.
Here he remained somewhat aloof from the staff but
gained some academic distinctions. He also worked
part-time during this period in the office of Paul
Kruchen, a tutor at the Highschool, to gain some
practical experience. When war broke out in 1914
Scharoun volunteered for military service but was not
called up until 1915. By this time Paul Kruchen had
been appointed district architect for rebuilding in East
Prussia and he reserved Scharoun as his site architect,
thus allowing him to complete his military service in
this capacity and to survive a war in which both of his
brothers were killed. Although most of the projects he
worked on were controlled by Kruchen, he did produce a few designs of his own in a sort of traditional
vernacular style.

5:1 The Utopian Period

At the end of the First World War German architecture passed through a phase of great hope, ferment and fantasy, which left a profound mark on Scharoun. The works of this period have been summed up, rather unsatisfactorily, under the general title of Expressionism. This tends to suggest links with movements in the other arts as well as in architecture which extend back into the prewar period. It seems superficially attractive as a category but encircles far too large a range of events to avoid being misleading. I prefer to use the term 'Utopian period' because it is more specific than the term 'Expressionism' to the intellectual atmosphere of postwar Germany, an atmosphere which had arguably more to do with political and social events than with questions of architectural style.

Germany was in a state of extreme poverty and political chaos. But at the same time the sudden relief from years of oppression and danger, combined with the conviction that this had been the war to end wars, resulted in a rash of Utopian idealism. Troops who had left home four years earlier laughing and singing had returned broken and dispirited, with nothing to show for their pains but death and destruction. They were understandably cynical of their leaders and of the political system that had caused the war, and they were idealistic about the socialism which they saw as the key to a new and better world. Dada, symptomatic of the intellectual climate, had been born in Zurich during the war, and it now spread to Berlin and Hannover. The Dadaists attacked convention, enraged the bourgeoisie by playing out practical jokes at an alarming scale, and leapt blindly into the unknown with their work in the visual and verbal arts, rejecting all aesthetic formulae and exploiting chance techniques.

For architects it was a time of great promise but few commissions. There was obviously much rebuilding to be done but economic collapse postponed it, and they were left to dream and plan ahead unhampered by practical and economic realities. This enforced idleness encouraged a spate of intellectual speculation, already likely in such a situation of turmoil and uncertainty. Cultural, political, philosophical and religious theories of all kinds were exchanged and discussed, and the most improbable sounding hypotheses were considered seriously. German intellectual life became a melting-pot for new and old ideas so that, far from being marked by one particular flavour or philosophy, the period is exceptional for the number and extremity of diverse views held. Disillusionment and disenchantment with the status quo had left a kind of spiritual vacuum. Great changes had been wrought, Europe had experienced destruction at a hitherto un-precedented scale. Now anything could happen; there was room for a new society, a better society, and for a new architecture. The past was best forgotten; the present was difficult; hopes were ever pinned on the future.

Today in our profession [wrote Bruno Taut] we cannot actually build, but we can seek and proclaim. We do not want to stop searching for that which, some time later can be crystallised, or to stop calling on comrades to walk with us the rough path, comrades who realise with profound humility that everything contemporary is only the earliest dawn, and who with self negating devotion prepare themselves for the rising of a new sun. A call goes out to all those who have faith in the future.[6]

Taut's call did not pass unheard. Young artists and architects in Berlin forgot their differences and united in the common conviction that 'the political revolution must be used to liberate art from decades of regimentation'. They set up the *Arbeitsrat für Kunst* ('Work Council for the Arts') to testify to their unity of purpose and to spread their ideas. A famous circular of 1919 runs:

Art and the people must form an entity. Art shall no longer be a luxury of the few but should be enjoyed and experienced by the broad masses. The aim is an alliance of the arts under the wing of a great architecture.[7]

The organisation was directed by Gropius, Behne and Klein. Among its associates were Poelzig, Mendelsohn, Bartning, the Taut brothers and of course Scharoun. He was not a central figure in the movement since he lived throughout that period in Insterburg and the focus of activity was Berlin. He was, however, a member of Bruno Taut's *Gläserne Kette* ('Glass Chain'), a smaller association of friends in different parts of Germany who communicated with each other through an exchange of circular letters and sketches. Many of these letters and other documents have been preserved, and they recreate very succinctly the flavour of the period besides giving us a good idea of the way in which their authors' thoughts were moving. Here are some extracts from an article published by Adolf Behne in 1918:

Building . . . a word that should resound in us like a jubilant cry, which calls us to our most proper and highest vocation, has become such a commonplace triviality for us that its sound falls wearily to the ground.

Building . . . which ought to be the co-operative effort of many enthusiastic people who, out of their love for the world, add something new to it, something great and splendid, a work which towers far above the individual, has instead become merely an everyday matter. What should be ecstasy has become only a concern with money . . . only the art of building can play with the great existing wonders around us. It attracts the sun to where there should be glitter and sparkling, it places its building storeys high in the sky, angular or curvilinear, smooth or ornamented, blunt or sharp edged, light or dark – and there the elements work the stones. Birds fly between them, the rain drenches them, the wind dries them, the frost splits them. Architecture is the only art that deals directly with the elements. The formation of the world is a kind of building, and through individuals filled with love of mankind, humanity builds a self perfecting form of the world.

    ... Architects could accomplish a great deal even today if, in each project with which they are faced, they would express how wonderful it is to build. It is wrong for the architects to take refuge in the simple requirements of their tasks. For the artist is always more than his employer, and if he does not share this sentiment, he should change his profession. The truth is that architecture has become so hackneyed that its disciples, even when they are completely unhampered, do not produce anything different from what they ordinarily do for daily wages.[8]

This passage contains most of the recurrent themes found in these letters and publications. Above all else rises the fervent plea for creativity and spiritual expression unhampered by scientific rationalism or commercial pressures. One of the strongest outbreaks against rationalism comes, surprisingly, from Gropius:

What is architecture? Surely the crystallised expression of man's noblest thoughts, of his ardour, his human nature, his faith, his religion! That it once was! But who of those living at this time, cursed as it is with materialism, does still understand the all-embracing and cheering character of architecture? Why do we not wander through our streets and towns weeping with shame over such wastelands of ugliness![9]

Bruno Taut handles the subject somewhat more philosophically:

My conception of the world: ... (To make it mean something for oneself) – applied to the universe this can only mean that one seeks to transfigure all that is perceived as 'real', that is, to interpret it and to give it a form. The form is at first the anchoring element and then becomes the all-embracing crystal, the 'world structure'.

    All that in science is considered to be merely mechanical or materialistic is therefore superfluous and even harmful. Higher causality reveals itself in the bad results of technology as a whole. The forces of nature, subdued by mere cunning, take their revenge upon this theft in an obvious way: where there should be temple worship, there is industry with all its greed, slavery, misery and murder. Science as such shall not be done away with. Yet, it must transform and change itself in such a way that the 'exact' is permeated by the poetic, just as the most exact discipline, even in the simplest calculations for the sphere, is completely dependent on the quite metaphysical concept of infinity. Thus mathematics is really the same as metaphysics.[10]

Here is the same theme, explored by Scharoun:

Bruno Taut, illustration from *Alpine Architecture* 1919. Credit: Gerd Hatje Verlag.

Der
Monte Resegone 1876 m bei Lecco
am Comersee.
Aufbauten vorwiegend aus Glas

Bruno Taut, project for the Folkwang school, Hohenhagen estate, Hagen 1920. Credit: Gerd Hatje Verlag.

Can we enforce pure creativity through reflection and knowledge? No. The human being should be the centre, with our aspirations forming a lofty vault over us like the firmament. Knowledge that leads us on a narrow path does not satisfy us. If it does in any way lead us to infinity, it is to a measurable segment, to a 'finite' infinity, to disappointment because of our isolation. The intervals between remain vacuous. Lateral interpenetration, mutual support, are missing, and instead of arriving at a play of forces we arrive at a mechanisation of forces.

... We believe in everything (even in nothing as long as it is original,) and we exist!

Otherwise we would have to vegetate in the labyrinths of a botanical science of ideas.[11]

Scharoun's contact with the Glass Chain had a considerable effect on his development. He was about ten years younger than most of the leading figures and he belonged to a generation which came to its maturity during the war and its aftermath. The 'Utopian period' therefore fell across his career at a time when he was still establishing his fundamental aims and ideals, and he remained closer to the spirit of it in later life than did any of his colleagues. His socialism and his basic philosophy, including a belief in intuition and distrust of science, were founded during this period. He never forgot his commitment to an idea of community and

its architectural expression, which derive essentially from these years. The terms *Volkshaus* ('people's hall') and *Stadtkrone* ('town-crown') occur often in the writings and projects of Taut's circle. The community building was seen as the principal element in a town, a physical representation of the people and their aspirations, and the living evidence of unity between art and people. It was to be the crown of the town, the climax of the urban architectural statement, and was to have much the same sort of significance as the Gothic cathedral had in a medieval town – a model to which conscious reference was made. The parallel between this kind of thinking and Scharoun's concern in his theatre and concert hall designs with the communal event and with the 'correct organic relationship with the townscape' is evident enough. In his Marl school too the communal hall is given dramatic emphasis as the centre of a hierarchical concentric layout: it is very much the crown of the school. But though the social ideals expressed in his later work refer back to the Utopian period, the way in which they are given expression belongs to a later stage of his development and there is little architectural resemblance between the later buildings and the projects of this early period.

Hans Poelzig, project for the Festspielhaus, Saltzburg, 1920. Credit: Gerd Hatje Verlag.

After completing his military service in 1919 Scharoun set up in private practice in Insterburg, remaining there until '25. He built relatively little, receiving a few commissions for private houses, and devoting most of his energy to numerous competition designs. However, the character of his projects underwent a considerable change. At the beginning of '19 he was still

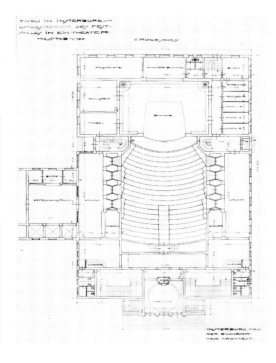

Project for a 'Tivoli' theatre at Insterburg, 1919, plan, (right) and elevations.

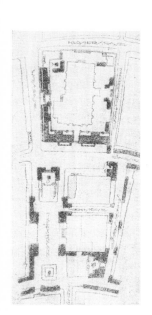

Project for the rebuilding of the Cathedral square at Prenzlau, 1919, plan and perspective sketch.

Wassili Luckhardt. Project for a religious building, 1920. Credit: Gerd Hatje Verlag.

designing very traditional buildings, rather rigid and classical in their planning. He gained his first competition success in that year with a plan for rebuilding the cathedral square at Prenzlau. This scheme, which was awarded first prize, is also classical in its planning but the suggested elevation treatment of the houses, a curious series of stepped arches, is somewhat unusual.

The Glass Chain correspondence became at times more specifically architectural in its concerns than is suggested by the documents already quoted. Bruno Taut and the Luckhardt brothers in particular were looking for some sort of new form language, and found inspiration in natural crystals and in forms implied by movement. Both of these subjects are covered in the following circular letter by Wassili Luckhardt:

I have in front of me a metallic geode broken out of its matrix. Many, many pyramids and prismatic shapes have, as it were, grown out of their matrix, and they sparkle and shine in the sunlight. Each one is different in size and shape, although each was formed according to the same laws. Do they not right away give the impression of architectural creations? And these creations, do they not seem to ask for man's shaping hand, which can build a significant whole out of the chaos of these elemental forms?

Does not this return to primary forms offer a possibility to arrive at certain basic architectural shapes which in their direct expressive power convey the impression of earth-grown configurations? The rock, the plant etc., are they not also made up of basic crystals?

My impressions of nature derived from phenomena of movement. I think that every work of art, and therefore of architecture, which aspires to be a replica of the cosmos must also have such movement in it. Because 'everything is in flux'.

This is marvellous; I can imagine that in a building freely set in nature the masses do not remain quiescent next to each other but push against and through each other with powerful dynamic movements, and that various lines of motion intersect each other or conflict (as for instance in Feininger's pictures). This occurs, however, in such a way – and this seems important to me – that nevertheless in the end everything is balanced and equilibrium is maintained; that is to say that every movement is met by an equally strong countermovement, so that no section of the building might threaten to overturn another. Perhaps the result would be that such buildings will have an ideal centre of gravity ...[12]

Taut and the Luckhardts produced sketches of possible projects which were circulated along with the correspondence. Usually these were impressions of extraordinary buildings in elevation, buildings that often had neither plans nor functions. Scharoun produced two competition projects in '20 in which he attempted to put the sort of crystalline shapes suggested by Taut and the Luckhardts to practical use. The first, a cultural centre in Gelsenkirchen entitled Mankind is Good (Scharoun liked to give his projects titles throughout his life), has a layout based on symmetry

and axes along classical lines, but the buildings are nonetheless differentiated from each other and the spaces very varied. The complex comes to a focus in an extraordinary crystalline tower on the community hall which is squat and pointed and strangely reminiscent of a wedding cake. Similar forms can be

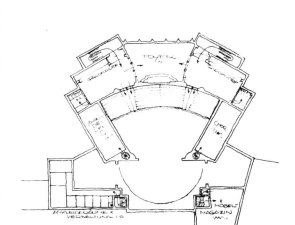

Project for the cultural centre at Gelsenkirchen, 1920, projection and plan of theatre.

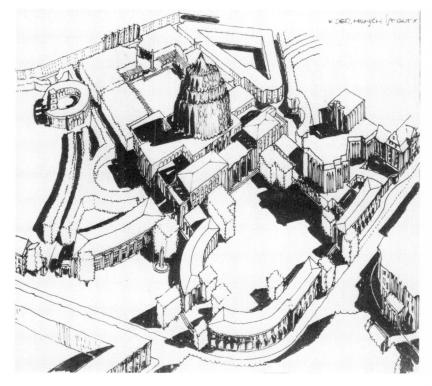

Wassili Luckhardt, 'Crystal on a sphere', project for a religious building, 1920. Credit: Gerd Hatje Verlag.

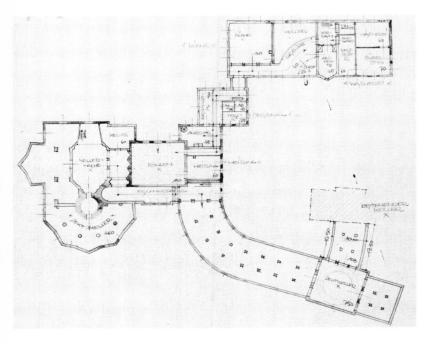

Project for an extension to premises of the firm Matheus Müller in Eltville, Rheinhessen, 1920, plan and perspective sketch.

found in the Luckhardts' work. The crystal had a strange, almost religious fascination for Taut's circle. It represented the ultimate in purity and simplicity, a unity of external form and internal structure. At the same time being transparent and reflective it mirrored the world, becoming inseparable from it though unviolated by it. The paradox was deeply felt: it became a kind of metaphysical puzzle. One is reminded of Blake's

To find infinity in a grain of sand
and eternity in an hour.

The shape of the other large building on the site, a theatre, is generated by the auditorium it contains (see plan), an early example of the formal articulation which later became predominant. The other competition scheme of '20 is even more surprisingly eclectic. It was a project for an extension to business premises and contains another version of the crystalline tower along with lower floors which repeat the crystalline form in shallow triangular projections provided with gothic arched windows. In the planning the heavy classical formalism has almost completely disappeared.

The 'crystalline' phase was short-lived. Forms which had so little functional relevance did not have lasting appeal. Perhaps in reaction against the classical formalism of his earlier years Scharoun next started

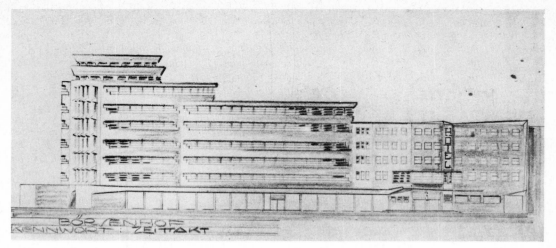

Project for the Stock Exchange building, Königsberg, 1922; elevation and ground floor plan.

to plan in free curves, deliberately ignoring all geometrical disciplines. He also became very interested in the idea of using movement as a generator of architectural form. This was a common theme among architects of the Utopian period, as Wassili Luckhardt's letter suggests, and the idea had been around for some time. It probably had its origins in prewar Italian futurism and it had found a more specifically architectural expression in Mendelsohn's wartime sketches, which had been influential. Scharoun produced sketches which were similar to those of Mendelsohn both in content and in style, suggesting a certain debt. However, Mendelsohn's sketches and those of other Utopian architects concerned buildings in elevation

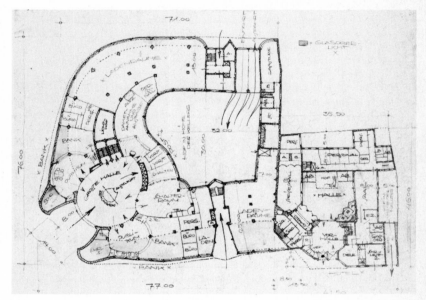

with soaring forms that had a purely visual significance. Scharoun tried as well to express movement at a more practical level by using circulation as a generator in plan. This resulted in a strange curvaceous style that is best represented by his competition entry for the Stock Exchange building at Königsberg of '22 entitled Zeittakt. Here the banks on the ground floor are designed around circular flow patterns, and the corridors of the upper floors are tapered in sympathy with diminishing traffic.

This building was probably the best example of this kind of planning that was produced at that time, but it was not produced in isolation and Scharoun cannot definitely be accredited with the initial idea. One certain and considerable influence on him was Hugo Häring and, although this only really became apparent much later, there is enough similarity between

Scharoun's Stock Exchange building and a railway station designed by Häring in the previous year to suggest a definite link even at this stage. Häring's station is planned in sweeping curves like the Stock Exchange building but what is more significant is that it was evidently planned with the same sort of intention – a response to circulation flow.

Hugo Häring (1882–1958) was a lifelong friend of Scharoun. Besides being an architect he was also a theorist of considerable repute and held during the twenties a polemical position that is historically very important. Among all the theorists of the 'organic' school he produced the most consistent and complete

Left
Project for the Chicago Tribune competition, 1922, sketch.

Project for the Stock Exchange building, Königsberg, 1922. Upper floor plans.

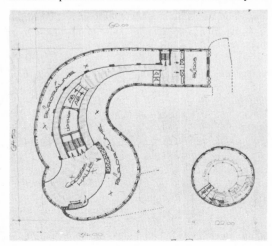

architectural philosophy, which he called 'the new building'. The basis of this theory, which will be dealt with in greater detail in a later chapter, is a rejection of geometrical aesthetics (rigidly rectangular planning, symmetry, proportion, etc.) in favour of a looser attitude towards form in which the shape of a building complex is derived from the various functions which it has to perform so that the form of the building becomes an expression of these functions, not in a metaphorical sense but as an inevitable consequence of closely following the brief.

Häring was eleven years older than Scharoun and had developed his theories by the mid-twenties, crystallising them in building with his famous farm buildings at Garkau, and in written work with his essay 'Wege zur Form' of '25. He became one of the most formidable opponents of the International Style and argued vigorously against Le Corbusier at the C.I.A.M. Congress of '28. However, he gradually lost ground: the lure of the simple, white, geometrical architecture was too strong. Here at last was a coherent style befitting the age of the machine and different from anything of the past. It was easily recognisable and imitable at a directly formal level. Häring's doctrine was, in contrast, too complex and too difficult to follow. Rather than advocating the adoption of a style or of a set of architectural elements such as Corbusier's five points, he was trying to establish a design method based on a return to fundamental principles. It was a very abstract approach, and unlike that of Le Corbusier it did not present a simple, coherent architectural image.

The relationship of Häring and Scharoun was never really that of master and pupil but rather, despite the age gap, a basic sympathy producing friendship and alliance. Although he must have been aware of Häring's theories in the mid-twenties, it is Scharoun's work of the thirties and later that most closely reflects them. This is partly because it was in the thirties, after most other modern movement architects had emigrated, that the two men saw most of each other. It is also partly because Häring's theory was concerned with the principles of architecture and a method of doing it rather than with a style, and this could hardly be adopted overnight.

Chapter 6: The Swing to Functionalism and the Growth of the International Style

The formal liberties of the Utopian period were on the whole exciting on paper but impossible to build. Those projects that did get built, like Mendelsohn's Einstein tower, were usually in exceptional situations, and

though they were widely admired their lack of functional relevance and the fact that often they were built in spite of materials rather than in response to them,* made such buildings unconvincing as examples to follow. Thus when in the mid-twenties the recovery of the economy allowed new building to take

* To be fair to Mendelsohn I ought to make it clear that the Einstein tower was in fact designed supposedly in response to the fluidity of poured concrete, but it was built in brick and rendered because the required shuttering technology to build it in concrete did not exist.

place at a reasonable scale it is hardly surprising that architects sobered up considerably and became more concerned with the possible.

One of the main tasks that they were faced with was the creation of low-cost mass housing. To be practical it had to be cheap and easy to build, which suggested simplicity, rectilinear geometry and repetition. An architectural style which fed on these conditions was obviously bound to succeed, particularly if it also broke with the confusion about choice of style that had become so acute and supported the general rejection of ornament. Le Corbusier created the necessary image, and it spread like wildfire in the guise of Functionalism or Rationalism. In fact none of the key buildings of the period, Le Corbusier's Villa Savoye, Mies's Barcelona Pavilion, Gropius's Bauhaus complex, stand up particularly well to strict functional analysis.

Erich Mendelsohn, Einstein tower at Potsdam, 1920.

Mies van der Rohe, Barcelona Exhibition Pavilion, 1929.

Corbusier. Villa Savoye at Poissy, 1929.

It was the image that they created that was important at the time rather than their functional performance.

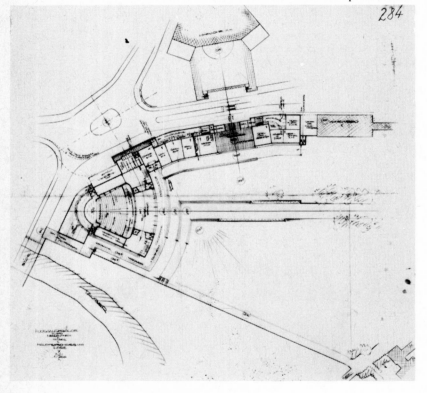

Scharoun became partly captivated by the International Style but was never entrenched in it. He took up the universal white surfaces, horizontal windows and mechanistic details, and from practical necessity his plans became more disciplined. However, he retained his own individual method of working, which was quite different from that of Le Corbusier or Mies or Gropius. The freehand planning unhampered by geometry, which was so evident in his 'curvaceous' period, remained as an underlying method even though the end results were more disciplined. It was only within such a loose framework that the kind of formal relationships that he sought could be found. He was gradually moving towards the confident expressive Functionalism of his later years. The formal articulation which was already evident in the 'crystalline' period became stronger and the use of circulation as a generator, as seen in the 'curvaceous' period, remained a perpetual possibility. Thus, although there is a great difference of style between Scharoun's buildings of the late twenties and those of the post-1918 period, this difference is not as fundamental as it might appear.

The change from the curvaceous style of the Stock Exchange building to the 'white architecture' of the late twenties took place gradually. The projects which Scharoun produced in '24 and '25 were transitional in character and it is really the Weissenhof house at Stuttgart that marks the establishment of the new style.

Project for public buildings at the Spa of Bad-Mergentheim, 1925, plan and elevation.

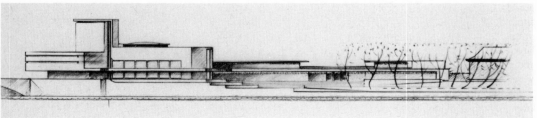

6:1 The Late 1920s and Early 1930s

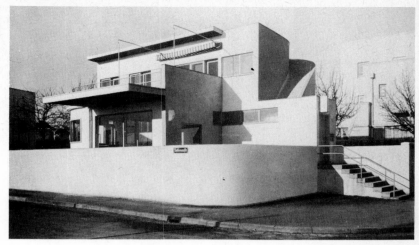

In '24 Scharoun was still working in private practice in Insterburg. In '25 he was invited to take up a professorship at the Breslau Arts Academy, of which Hans Poelzig had been director from 1903–16, being succeeded by August Endell. Endell's death caused a reshuffle of staff: the painter Oscar Moll succeeded Endell, and Adolf Rading became head of the architectural faculty. It was Rading who offered Scharoun the job. Scharoun accepted and taught at Breslau until '32. During that period he and Rading saw a great deal of each other, for a time they shared an office in Berlin, and there are superficial similarities between their works. Rading's block of flats for the Breslau Werkbund of '29 was quite different from Scharoun's in concept but bore a similar stylistic treatment, with similar 'marine' details. Whether Rading contributed significantly to Scharoun's development or not remains doubtful.

Despite spending much of his time in Breslau Scharoun did not lose contact with the architectural avant-garde which was still centred, as always, in Berlin. In '26 he joined the Ring, an organisation set up in the previous year to demonstrate solidarity against the planning policies of Ludwig Hoffmann, then Berlin city architect. The secretary of the Ring was Häring and its membership included nearly every contemporary German architect of note. Eventually they were successful in their purpose and Hoffmann was replaced by Martin Wagner. Wagner was a broad-minded man who believed in delegating much of his power to other architects. He saw his position as similar to that of an orchestral conductor, a sort of co-ordinator of individual efforts. It was Wagner who later commissioned Scharoun to plan Siemensstadt, and several other Berlin developments of that period were planned the same way.

Through his membership of the Ring Scharoun knew Mies, who was called upon in '27 to organise the Weissenhof exhibition for the Deutscher Werkbund and invited Scharoun to participate. The exhibition involved the building of an experimental suburb in Stuttgart with a variety of house and flat types designed by a selection of important architects. Most of the well known German architects, except Mendelsohn and Häring, contributed designs, as well as Le Corbusier and the Dutch architects J. J. P. Oud and Mart Stam. The only restriction imposed on them was the provision that all the buildings should have flat roofs.

Scharoun was given a corner plot on the downhill-facing south side of the site, on which to build a single detached house. He produced a structure in reinforced

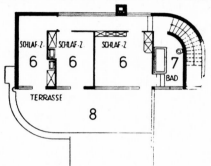

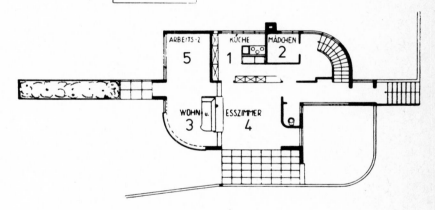

Prototype family house at the Weissenhof Exhibition, Stuttgart, 1927. Ground and first floor plans; 1, kitchen; 2, maid's room; 3, living-room; with 4, dining area, and 5, study area; 6, bedrooms; 7, bathroom; 8, roof terrace.

Top
View from the street.

concrete which combines an extraordinary mixture of ingredients. It has the same plain white surfaces and horizontal windows as most of its neighbours, but it also has a very broken up external form devoid of symmetry and a plan based on circular as well as rectilinear

Below
The living-dining space.

forms. The front of the house is made up of a series of intersecting planes set at right angles. This kind of conception was popular at the time: there are suggestions of it in Mies's Weissenhof block and more strongly in his famous Barcelona Pavilion of the following year. It came undoubtedly from the Dutch De Stijl movement and can be found in its most undiluted form in Rietveldt's Schröder house of '24. In Scharoun's hands the intersecting planes were not just an empty stylistic gesture, but a means of expressing the open south side of his house in contrast with the hard north-facing protective back wall which curves around to the entrance side as one continuous surface, articulating the spiral form of the staircase.

Although he was using many elements from the vocabulary of the International Style, his intentions were very different from those of the aesthetic purists who invented it. He took his cues from the site and the programme, and used whatever elements would answer to the various conditions he was building for. His aim was not a pleasing composition but rather the creation of a form expressive of its function irrespective of aesthetic considerations. He considered himself anti-aesthetic and at times this took on an almost Dadaist zeal. The Weissenhof house shows his willingness to mix formal ingredients in whatever configuration the task suggested, regardless of taste, and consequently it was one of the most controversial of the exhibits. Purists have always hated his work because

they find it so aesthetically iconoclastic.

The Weissenhof house was Scharoun's first important built work, and it marks the beginning of a very active and fruitful period in his career during which he quickly built up a considerable reputation. This period spans the years '27 to '33, coming to its end with the rise of the Nazis. In these years Scharoun built several apartment blocks, the most famous of which are those at Siemensstadt, on Hohenzollerndamm and on Kaiserdamm in Berlin, and that of the Werkbund exhibition in Breslau. He also produced several designs for house types of various kinds in various materials, for it was a time of great experimentation with new types of construction and new opportunities for flexibility. In '26 he worked on a project called 'the elastic ground plan', in '27 on a transportable wooden house, in '28 on a house type for a magazine, in '31 on various house types, in '32 on another transportable house and more house types, and in '33 on a project entitled 'the variable dwelling'. Between '27 and '33 he worked altogether on no less than forty-one projects for houses, house types or apartment blocks. In doing all these schemes Scharoun covered a great deal of ground and explored a very large number of planning possibilities, an experience which obviously contributed to his later ability to plan so freely and yet so well.

While working on the Weissenhof house in '27 Scharoun was also working on his first transportable

Apartment block on the Kaiserdamm, Berlin, 1929.

house, which was built for the German Garden and Industry Exhibition at Liegnitz. This was a single-storey timber-framed structure. It was planned on a rectangular grid in the interests of prefabrication. Such a predominant constructional discipline is rarely found in Scharoun's work as he normally determined his plan first and then set about finding a construction for it, allowing spatial values to dominate. However, even within the constraints of grid planning he managed to produce a remarkably free design with a surprising degree of formal and spatial articulation.

The accommodation is split up into three parts marked on the plan as 'working section', 'living section' and 'sleeping section'. These units are all more or less the same size and shape, and they are juxtaposed not in a classical-geometrical manner but in a way that allows the best interrelation of internal functions and simultaneously creates a pair of semi-enclosed garden spaces on opposite sides of the house. The link between the 'working section' and 'living section' allows the kitchen to have direct access to both entrance and dining area, while the link between the 'living section' and 'sleeping section' is much narrower. Only one passage need go through so the sleeping section is pushed over allowing a screened sunbathing area to be accommodated at the end of it. Thus, although the juxtaposition of the three sections may seem at first sight somewhat free and arbitrary, it turns out when examined closely to be a remarkably tight and specific arrangement.

On the public side of the house the main entrance and study next to it are projected by one grid unit, which serves partly to stress the entrance externally and partly to allow the 'working section' of the house to recede slightly and gain some privacy. The study also projects in the other plane beyond the living-room window, which both accommodates a sofa conveniently inside and begins to enclose the garden terrace outside. This suggestion of enclosure is taken further by the wooden screen supporting the roof of the covered part of the terrace, which was evidently meant to be trailed with climbing plants and cut off part of the garden from the approach side. The living-room window and garden terrace are placed of course on the south-facing side of the house, while bedroom and kitchen windows face east, the entrance, study and 'working section' west, and nothing at all north.

Within the three sections of the house functions are differentiated in a remarkably specific manner and furniture and cupboards are designed into the plan if not built in. We can tell from most house plans where the family will sleep and where they will wash, but in

Scharoun's plan we know too where they will eat and where they will sit on their sofa. We know where father will do the accounts and the children their homework. We know in surprising detail where cooking and washing will be done. We know also where the family will lie sunbathing and where they will sit outside in the shade. All of these things are provided for and designed into the plan: they generate the plan. As we examine it Scharoun's intentions become more and more obvious. The building was not conceived as a box and then divided up, nor was it based on an aesthetically pleasing formal layout, nor on a set of pleasing elevations, nor on a pure response to structure or construction: it was conceived rather as a series of functional spaces carefully interrelated, each with an orientation and degree of enclosure appropriate to its purpose. Thus already in '27 Scharoun's course was set, his priorities decided. In his post-1945 work his planning is freer and his stylistic vocabulary different but the fundamental values of his architecture are much the same.

Scharoun's position at the Breslau Arts Academy led to his playing an important part in the Breslau Werkbund exhibition of '29, and it was there that he

Timber-framed modular house for the German Garden and Industry Exhibition at Liegnitz, 1927–8.
Entrance side.

Ground floor plan; 1, working section; 2, living section; 3, sleeping section; 4, entrance; 5, kitchen; 6, maid's room; 7, laundry; 8, drying room; 9, study; 10, living-dining; 11, children's bedroom; 12, parents' bedroom; 13, wardrobes; 14, worktable; 15, bathroom; 16, sun terrace.

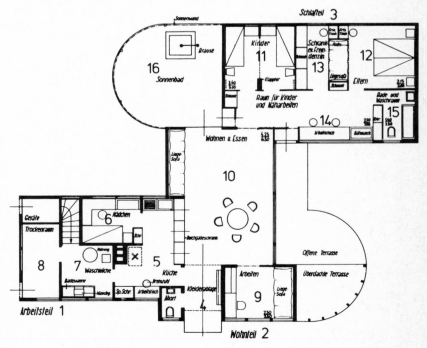

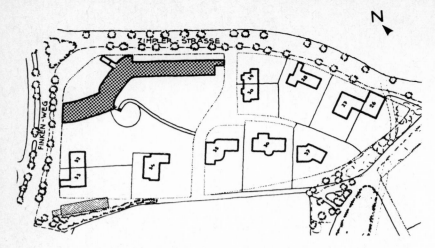

Apartment block at the Breslau Werkbund Exhibition, 1929. Site plan.

built his first sizeable building, a *Wohnheim*, an experimental block of flats somewhat like a hotel having one and two person flats without kitchens and a communal hall and restaurant on the ground floor. The marine imagery of this building has already been commented upon – it still seems remarkable today. But perhaps even more remarkable is the planning. As one might expect, the various parts are articulated according to their functions. Thus two wings, one containing one person flats and the other two person flats, extend out-

wards from opposite ends of a communal hall in a linear arrangement. Each wing has two floors of flats but through an ingenious split-level arrangement both floors relate to one corridor. The shorter wing contains the two person flats and has a restaurant on the ground floor. In addition to the main structure, a block of lavatories is tacked on to the rear side of the building at ground floor level and a curved wall which retains a level-change in the garden sticks out from the front. This wall grows into a partially shaded sun terrace and

Ground floor plan.

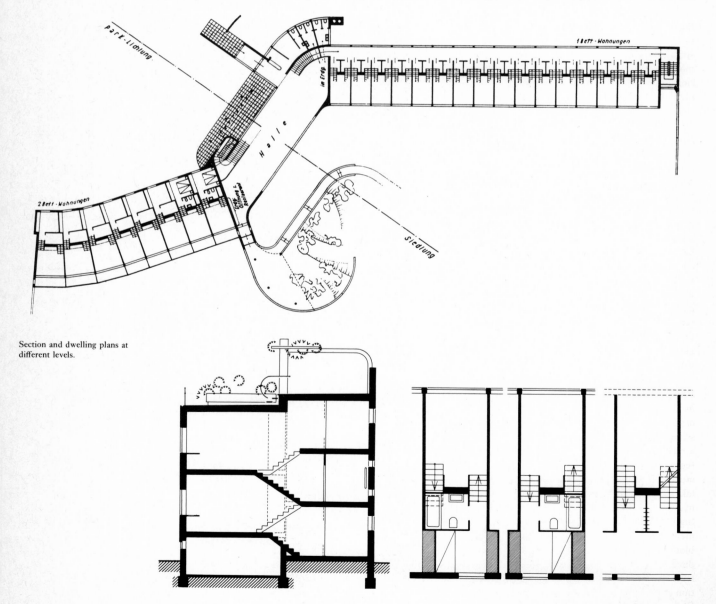

Section and dwelling plans at different levels.

[72]

serves the further function of dividing that part of the garden related to the restaurant from the part related to the communal hall and the long wing containing the one person flats.

Perhaps the most unorthodox feature of the plan is the way in which the building is cranked at either end of the communal hall. The angle changes have no geometrical significance: they were chosen purely to get the appropriate juxtaposition of parts on the site. Scharoun was using the form of his building to control the remaining spaces around it. In front of the building he created two tranquil garden spaces separated by the sun terrace wall, while behind it he created a harder, more public space, which served as an outdoor extension to the restaurant. By glazing the communal hall on both sides he highlighted its significance as a transitional space between front and back.

This attitude towards space distinguishes Scharoun's building from all the others produced at the Breslau exhibition, and indeed from International Style buildings elsewhere. Whereas Le Corbusier, Mies, Gropius and their followers were producing beautifully balanced geometrical plans which had considerable aesthetic charm on paper, Scharoun's plan is wilfully untidy – as a geometrical pattern it is not attractive. Elements are not always integrated into the basic geometry of the plan, instead they are often added on in an almost casual manner, where necessary. Each staircase is treated as a separate case; level-changes abound; complexity is welcomed. But although these things look untidy on paper they work remarkably well in reality. Good spatial relationships do not necessarily imply precise geometrical relationships, as anyone who has visited an unplanned medieval town will know.

The unusual differentiation of spaces found in the Breslau building occurs again at Siemensstadt. When in '30 Martin Wagner gave Scharoun the task of co-ordinating the overall layout Scharoun chose for himself a small corner of the site cut off from the rest by a railway, a plot which many architects would have regarded as difficult. He chose it because it suggested, more than other less restricted plots that he might have taken instead, certain moves that he was willing to make. He welcomed a site that demanded a reaction. Significantly, Scharoun was the only architect at Siemensstadt who produced neither a run of parallel blocks nor blocks lining the edges of roads. He produced instead three different blocks treated in different ways and juxtaposed to produce a differentiation of spaces not to be seen elsewhere in the scheme. Once again it does not look very seductive on plan, but

the spaces created in practice are convincing and Scharoun's corner of Siemensstadt has a stronger sense of place than any other part of the site.

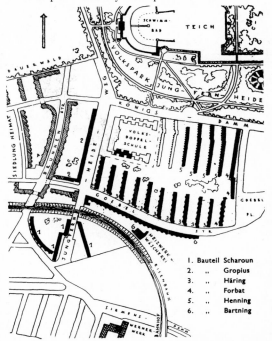

Top. Apartment block at the Breslau Werkbund Exhibition, 1929.
View of south-east wing from roof terrace.

View from roof terrace over central hall.

1. Bauteil Scharoun
2. „ Gropius
3. „ Häring
4. „ Forbat
5. „ Henning
6. „ Bartning

Siemensstadt housing development, 1930. Site plan.

Views of the area in Siemensstadt designed by Scharoun.

Project for two-storeyed terraced housing in Berlin, 1931, plans of ground and first floors.

First Floor

Ground Floor *i.M. 1:100*

At Siemensstadt and Breslau it is the handling of external spaces around Scharoun's buildings that is most exceptional; internal spaces are generally parallel sided and subservient to rectangular geometry. This is also true of nearly everything else that Scharoun designed between '27 and '33. Curves can often be found in the plans, but they are not generally an inevitable part of the planning and could be straightened out without disastrous effects on functional performance. A terrace of two-storey houses designed for a Berlin exhibition of '30 is typical. The curved walls add

interest and work well but they are not fundamentally necessary and the rest of the plan is rectangular. The main difference between this terrace and those of Mies or Gropius is its looseness and the evidence of design from the inside outwards by assembling rooms, in contrast with the more usual International Style policy of dividing up a simple shell.

At Breslau, Scharoun recognised that the site suggested more than one pair of axes and responded by cranking his building, as has already been described, but the building is nonetheless essentially linear and the internal spaces are parallel sided. Had he been faced with the same brief twenty years later he would almost certainly have contrasted the different axes within the building to produce tapering spaces where they could be used advantageously – this is a predominant theme in all his postwar work. But in '29 he had not yet discovered the real advantages of diverging from the rectangle within buildings, although there are strong hints that he was quite willing to do so if convenient. The turning-point came in '33 with the design of the Schminke house, Scharoun's own favourite among his house projects and his last building before the Nazi clamp-down.

Fritz Schminke was a wealthy industrialist with adventurous tastes, from Löbau in Saxony. He had a plot of land near his works and commissioned Scharoun to build him a luxury house there. The approach road bordered the site on the south side, but the best view available was towards the NE. Scharoun decided to build the house at the south end of the site where the public side of it could be close to the road and, at the same time, the house would form a screen between the road and the main part of the garden. This policy resulted in a conflict as far as outlook was concerned: the view out was on one side and sunlight came from the other. Making a virtue of necessity Scharoun decided to employ the idea he had exploited in some of the Siemensstadt flats, of having rooms with windows on both façades. This turned out to be not only satisfactory but highly convenient. The ideal of continuity with the garden through the largest possible windows could be obtained without uncontrollable solar heat gain in summer, the south side being provided with smaller horizontal windows, and the conservatory could be placed on the sunny side without obstructing the view.

The house, being mainly one room thick, became in consequence long and thin, making a more effective screen between garden and road than would have been the case with a more compact arrangement. But perhaps the most significant aspect of the planning is the

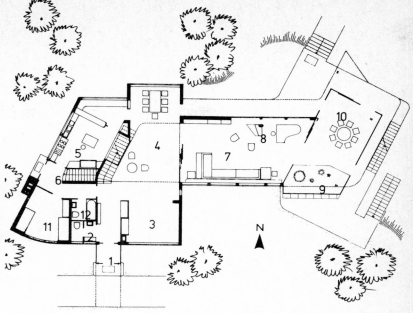

Schminke House, Löbau, Saxony,
1932–3. Ground floor plan;
1, entrance from drive;
2, cloakroom; 3, studio; 4, hall and
dining area; 5, kitchen; 6, cellar
steps; 7, living-room; 8, hearth;
9, conservatory; 10, solarium;
11, bedroom; 12, bathroom.

Top left
View from garden.

Left and bottom left.
Living area by day and by night.

way the two axes, suggested by orientation and view,
marry inside the house to produce some very unorthodox spatial effects. The glass sided solarium at the
outer end of the living-room is directly orientated towards the view but the main part of the living-room
falls along the east to west axis with a built-in sofa on
the sunny south side. The sofa relates diagonally to
large windows in line with the view, and this diagonal
shift is echoed in the relation of the living-room to the
solarium. Since the sofa already faces the view a very

minimal hearth is related to it by being placed in line
with the view, and the space between this hearth and
the sliding screen of the solarium turns out to be a convenient shape for the accommodation of the grand
piano.

First floor plan; 1, master
bedroom; 2, bathroom; 3, void
over hall; 4, 5, 6, bedrooms;
7, wardrobes in passage;
8, terrace.

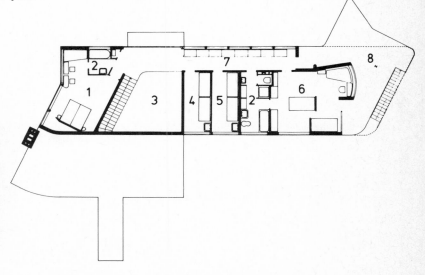

At the other end of the house the change in angle is taken up in the principal staircase, which is slanted in sympathy with the general direction of circulation movement towards the long end of the house. The angle of the stair takes up the transition between the axis of entry on the ground floor and the axis of the upstairs corridor. It also presents a strong visual suggestion of movement in the same direction on the ground floor, and whether one is actually on the staircase or just walking beside it one is guided around towards the right. This use of a staircase to suggest and control a change in circulation direction was a highly significant development and it later became a dominant feature of Scharoun's planning vocabulary.

The Schminke house demonstrates an attitude towards space quite unlike that of any of Scharoun's contemporaries. Free planning with sliding screens and continuity with the outside through large areas of glass were common themes of the time, but nobody handled them quite as Scharoun did. The architects of the De Stijl movement had discovered that a house did not necessarily have to be a box and that windows did not necessarily have to be perforations in a wall, and these themes were effectively exploited by Mies in his Barcelona Pavilion of '28 where the walls are treated as freestanding planes. The spaces produced flowed in and out in a disarming way; the tyranny of the box was seen to be broken. But Mies's assemblage of planes was very much an abstract composition and the Barcelona Pavilion could hardly be considered a tightly functional building. Scharoun's conception of space demonstrated the same freedom but it also demonstrated a close response to, and dependence on site, function and orientation.

Perhaps the best International Style building to contrast with the Schminke house is Le Corbusier's Villa Savoye at Poissy, which was built to a similar brief. The essential difference between the two buildings is that while the Schminke house is inextricably based on its particular site and would make little sense if transplanted to a different one, the Villa Savoye could have been built on any reasonably open site anywhere. It stands isolated in the middle of its plot, showing no control whatsoever of the surrounding space.

The form of the Schminke house was determined by a series of close responses to function as Scharoun interpreted it, and the elevations are the end result of the planning process. Windows occur in varying positions and in varying shapes and sizes according to the particular requirements of view and lighting. The resulting composition is untidy and to some people ugly. The Villa Savoye was, on the other hand, composed very carefully according to strict principles of proportion and geometrical interrelationship. The elevations were set up to be visually harmonious – and the result is a building of striking beauty and grace. Both the Schminke house and the Villa Savoye are in different ways masterpieces but they do not solve the same problems or succeed in the same ways. The visual perfection of the Villa Savoye and the untidy responsiveness of the Schminke house are mutually incompatible: Le Corbusier's geometrical disciplines could not accommodate the kind of conception that Scharoun sought, which explains Scharoun's disdain for aesthetic principles generally.

The contrast between the two buildings highlights the contrast between the International Style and Häring's 'new building', for the Schminke house is a good example of 'new building' in everything except its white rendered surfaces. So far I have kept off the complex subject of Häring's theory and its derivation since this requires extensive coverage, being an area of architectural history that is neither well known nor well understood. However, an appreciation of Häring's position, which was also Scharoun's position very largely, is very necessary for a real understanding of Scharoun's contribution to architectural history, and therefore I shall return in the next chapter to the mid-twenties and the conflict between Häring and Le Corbusier.

But I must not leave Scharoun's biography in the air. The Schminke house was the last building he produced in '33. The Nazis condemned modern architecture as degenerate and conditions gradually became more and more unpleasant for all those involved in the

Le Corbusier. Villa Savoye, Poissy, 1929.

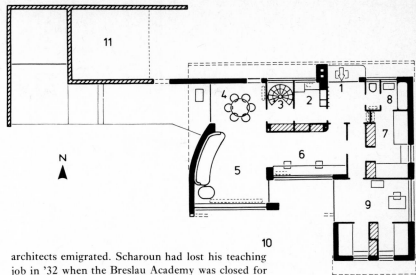

modern movement. After a few half-hearted attempts to compromise with the Nazis most of the important architects emigrated. Scharoun had lost his teaching job in '32 when the Breslau Academy was closed for

House for the landscape architect Hermann Mattern at Bornim, near Potsdam, 1934, plan; 1, entrance from street; 2, kitchen; 3, cellar stairs; 4, dining area; 5, living area; 6, workroom/study; 7, parents' bedroom; 8, bathroom; 9, room for young child and au pair girl; 10, garden; 11, garage. Living-rooms face south and bedrooms east, bedrooms of minimum size to allow more space elsewhere, as this was a low budget scheme; a prominent design consideration was that the child at play inside or outside could be supervised from both living-room and workroom.

View from garden.

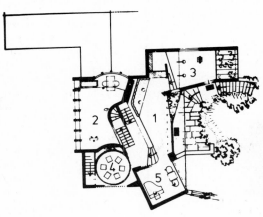

political reasons. Under the Nazis he lost also the chance of obtaining public commissions or of participating in competitions, for he was seen as a 'culture-bolshevist', and he therefore had to rely entirely on private clients. He considered emigration but felt too closely tied to his country and its culture. Significantly Häring too remained in Germany, teaching at an art

House for the painter Oskar Moll, Berlin, 1937; upper ground and first floor plans; 1, living-room looking out on garden side; 2, studio on street side; 3, studio; 4, dining-room; 5, music room; 6, 7, 8, 9, bedrooms; 10, bathroom.

View from garden.

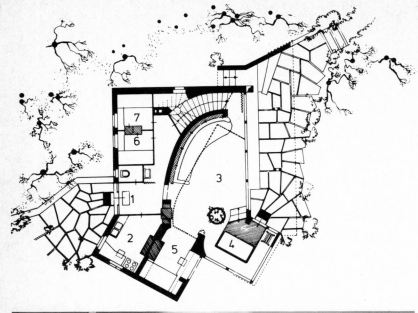

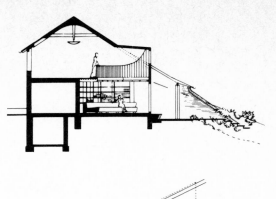

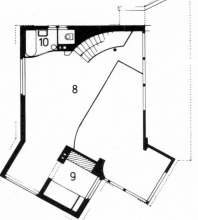

school. Those who believed in an International Style could work at an international level, but those who believed in specific architectural solutions based on the particular locality and culture involved were less likely to do so. Scharoun felt too that outside Germany he would not be understood – perhaps he was right. In any case he thought that the Hitler regime could not last for ever and determined to stick it out. I need hardly emphasise that his political beliefs could scarcely have been further from those of the Nazis and that he never compromised himself by building for them.

Moller House, Brandenburg, 1937; ground floor plan, first floor plan and section; 1, entrance hall; 2, kitchen; 3, living-room commanding view of lake; 4, dining area in floor well; 5, study; 6, 7, bedrooms; 8, gallery; 9, bedroom; 10, bathroom.

View from garden.

Mohrmann house, Berlin, 1939, roadside view.

He attracted enough commissions between '33 and '43 to keep him in business, and he also managed to give employment to various young architects outlawed by the Nazis. In this decade he built no less than fifteen private houses and produced designs for a few more. He also planned a few small housing projects, and between '41 and '43 worked on a research programme for laundry design. After '43 the war made private building almost impossible and Scharoun eked out a living for a couple of years without designing anything. For a time he had a job clearing bomb damage. His only creative refuge was a series of watercolours showing rather grandiose and abstract architectural conceptions. These are the works of frustration, private dreams to sustain a sensitive mind in a crumbling world. They have been seen by some critics as an accumulation of formal capital in preparation for later years, and they have also been used too often to justify the claim that Scharoun was an Expressionist, more concerned with wild dreams than with functional realities. But within his own terms Scharoun was a strict functionalist. Never in his mature work did he produce

Pflaum house, Falkensee, near Berlin, 1935.

a scheme based on an idea plucked, so to speak, from the blue and unrelated to the situation in hand. This period of inaction at the end of the war is a convenient point at which to break my biographical narrative in favour of an excursion into the theory and derivation of 'new building', and I shall continue the biographical survey thereafter.

Hoffmeyer house, Bremerhaven, 1935, view from garden.

Chapter 7: 'New Building' versus the International Style

We have seen in previous chapters how the social and political atmosphere of Germany at the end of the First World War produced a state of Utopian fantasy among German architects, and how this was superseded in the mid-twenties by a more realistic and practical approach. We have seen also how these conditions were favourable to the establishment of the International Style. Many historians have confused these two issues, assumed that the International Style was synonymous with Functionalism and interpreted the events of the period as a swing from Expressionism to Functionalism. When we compare the wild sketches of the immediate postwar period with the 'white architecture' of a decade later, and do not analyse either too carefully, this seems a satisfactory description. However, if we look less superficially and try to distill the essence of Expressionism or of Functionalism, confusion sets in.

Are not all buildings to some extent functional, and do not all buildings express something? Why in any case should one ism exclude the other, cannot we have Expressive Functionalism? The confusion of these issues has been caused to a large extent by a tremendous bias on the part of leading historians, particularly Nikolaus Pevsner, towards the International Style, and by their failure to take its opponents seriously. They showed their bias by erring in two directions. Firstly they refused to recognise that many of the architects they considered Expressionist were not in fact indulging in whimsical individual expression but operating quite rationally from unusual premises. Secondly they refused to admit the irrationality of the International Style and the fact that it was founded on subjective rather than absolute values. They therefore set up the International Style as the ultimate architecture and tended to dismiss anything that did not conform to it as Expressionist. Expressionism then became a sort of waste paper basket for the parts of the historical jigsaw that did not seem to fit and it ended up containing an extraordinary range of ideologies, including some like that of Häring that are essentially Functionalist in nature. Even when used in its narrowest sense to refer to events in German and Dutch architecture between about 1912 and '25, Expressionism covers an extraordinary range of disparate tendencies, united only by a rejection of the orthodox. Used in a wider sense, as for instance by Pevsner, to include even some of the post-1945 work of Le Corbusier it remains meaningful only as a category of exclusion rather than inclusion, and is more useful to those trying to dismiss the architecture included in it than to those trying to understand it.

Functionalism is a much more useful and definable term. Surely it indicates a close response by a building to the purpose which it is destined to serve, so that this purpose can be served as effectively as possible. Strict Functionalists believe that all aspects of a building, including those concerned with its visual meaning and aesthetic value, must be related to the purpose served.

Now Functionalism is by no means the monopoly of the International Style: it has been around since Vitruvius at least. It is even doubtful whether any of the key architects of the International Style were strict Functionalists: they were all too concerned with achieving aesthetic purity. Le Corbusier's shocking statement about a house being a machine for living in has become the catch phrase of generations, but we must remember that according to Le Corbusier architecture was, at the same time:

... the masterly correct and magnificent play of masses brought together in light: cubes, cones, spheres or pyramids are the great primary forms which light reveals to advantage. These are the beautiful forms, the most beautiful forms.[13]

At heart Le Corbusier was always unashamedly concerned with aesthetics. He was, after all, an important painter as well as an architect, and though he cannot be accused of producing buildings based on two dimensions instead of three, his buildings are nonetheless pure self-contained units just as his paintings are contained by and composed within their frames. He never tried to blend his buildings into their sites and, as Wright pointed out, he was at pains to detach his buildings from the ground rather than letting them be a part of it.

Le Corbusier also played a fundamental role in redefining some of the principles of classical architecture with his theories of proportional and geometrical interrelationships. His drawings of Renaissance buildings showing the geometrical breakdown of façades are well known. Le Corbusier's interest in classical architecture was shared by Mies and Gropius. Significantly all three architects worked during the early years of the century at the office of Peter Behrens – arguably a neo-classicist and a disciple of Schinkel. Mies's neo-classicism and his debt to Schinkel have been widely acknowledged, but Gropius's neo-classical bias has been largely ignored. Nevertheless, a preference for simplicity, symmetry and formality is obvious in most of his planning and his elevations all tended to be carefully composed and proportioned. On the façade of his famous Werkbund building of 1914, which is very formal and perfectly symmetrical, one can even find reduced classical pilasters with capitals in the brick-work.

It was Le Corbusier, rather than Mies or Gropius, who really set up the International Style through the influence of certain key works in the late-twenties, of which the aforementioned Villa Savoye at Poissy is perhaps the most important. This building must have seemed stunningly original when it was built in '29,

all objected to the 'white architecture' on essentially Functionalist grounds. Wright objected to the lack of response to siting and materials, and Lethaby spoke mockingly of 'Ye olde modern style' and supported 'sound expressive building', claiming, 'there is no per-sistence in anything else'. Häring shared the views of the other two and went a good deal further. He recog-nised the essentially neo-classical nature of the Inter-

Le Corbusier. Villa Savoye, Poissy, 1929.

and irresistible as a model. Even now it is very impres-sive and only its details and fittings remind one that it is fifty years old. With this seductive image and a list of five points to follow, with which one could sup-posedly recreate it, Le Corbusier had no difficulty in recruiting followers. The Villa Savoye was certainly the vehicle for new constructional ideas and a new formal vocabulary, but above all else it was a master-piece of visual composition in three dimensions. Its simplicity, whiteness, and total lack of ornament all enhance its qualities as abstract sculpture, qualities that would suffer if for example the natural finishes of materials were expressed. Certain aspects of the building could be considered Functionalist, but its conception was firmly wedded to abstract aesthetics.

This fact was recognised at the time by Frank Lloyd Wright, W. R. Lethaby and Häring simultaneously. They were all builders rather than painters, and they

national Style and revived many of the old arguments that had raged between Neo-classicists and Gothic Revivalists in the nineteenth century, arguments con-cerning the validity of abstract aesthetics. He stood for the responsive solution to an architectural problem as opposed to the imposed solution, and he set up the theory of 'new building' against the International Style and, more particularly, against the principles of Le Corbusier.

I think it no exaggeration to call Häring the lost key to the twenties. Despite the fact that he built little, had few followers, and lost his battle against Le Corbusier, he has earned an important place in architectural his-tory. His historical value lies in the fact that he forms a sort of counterweight to the International Style, standing for the set of ideas that it rejected. Because his ideology did not catch on, and because he stayed in Germany during the Nazi period, he lapsed into an obscurity in the thirties from which he never re-emerged. He became something of a recluse, continuing to develop his own philosophical theories and building nothing but a few houses. After the war he had become obscure enough to be totally omitted from Bruno Zevi's *Towards an Organic Architecture* in which, arguably, he should have been a key figure. He eventually died after a long illness in '58 and his work was rediscovered in the early sixties when the International Style began to fall out of favour.

Häring is the theorist behind Scharoun, but Scharoun was never Häring's pupil: their relationship was one of friendship and alliance. Their works are outwardly different in character: it is at the level of principles and method that one finds great similarities. The extent of Scharoun's debt to Häring is impossible to estimate, but even if it is smaller than I suppose Häring can contribute a great deal to our understanding of Scharoun, because he wrote what Scharoun chose to leave unwritten. Just as Häring provides us with a theoretical background for Scharoun so Scharoun developed and proved the worth of Häring's theoretical ideas. But you can best judge for yourself how principles relate to practice. I have described already a cross-section of Scharoun's work and now I shall describe Häring's theory, leaving my reader to perceive for himself the links between the two.

'New building' falls within the compass of the organic tradition, and indeed Häring also referred to 'organic building'. He was probably influenced by Frank Lloyd Wright whose work had been published in Germany as early as 1910. Häring shared with Wright a number of fundamental concepts: in both men's theories one finds the idea that function should generate form as it does in nature so that, as Wright put it, 'form and function are one'. One finds also in both theories an emphasis on part to whole, the part should have an identity of its own which is yet contained within the whole. In both theories architecture (or building) is considered in the broadest possible context, each building being seen as a unique case inextricably based on its particular site and function, and an integral part of the life which it serves. The building becomes a part of the landscape and, conversely, the landscape is seen as a form of architecture.

Beyond these broad similarities the theories of Häring and Wright differ considerably. Wright was always ready to indulge himself in styling and ornament, whereas Häring shared with his European colleagues a conviction that pure functional forms had the highest cultural value:

Today we demand utilitarian objects without adornments, not disguised as something else, free from masking, incrustations. They may nevertheless be noble and exquisite objects, highly valuable products; exquisite quality can be attained without senseless twisting and bending, impressed patterns and the like, which only infringe the objects' essential rights.

There is no worse enemy of the form dictated by purpose than applied art. The causes may vary, but the effect is always the same; namely, violation of the utilitarian object. If we realise this today a great change must have taken place in us, since in thousands of years of the production of artefacts this viewpoint has rarely exercised any effective influence. I see in this fact a moral gain by the present, I regard it as the sign of a new evolving culture. It can also be looked at differently. It may be said that we have become rationalistic, we no longer attach any value to having an Apollo striding across the Greek landscape with his lyre depicted on our teapots.

We have discovered that purely functional things have forms which can satisfy us in terms of expression, and indeed some forms created solely out of functional necessity become more satisfying in terms of expression as they become functionally purer, and that this kind of expression resulted in a new aesthetic. We acknowledged the expressive qualities found in machines, ships, cars, aircraft and thousands of other objects and instruments.[14]

There are of course photographs of ships, cars, aircraft, etc., in *Vers une architecture*. Häring's point of view in these matters was shared by Le Corbusier and also by the Bauhaus architects. There was a great solidarity against the meaningless perpetuation of historical styles that was still rife. Even in '27 the architecture and views of the modern movement were still very avant-garde:

The architects of the Weissenhof housing project had the greatest of difficulty in finding tables and chairs for their rooms, to say nothing of cupboards, although in Stuttgart and elsewhere thousands and thousands of tables and chairs were standing about in furniture stores and these tables and chairs would undoubtedly have satisfied the objective demands made upon them. The only drawback was their appearance.[15]

Over the design of utilitarian objects Häring seems to have been in perfect agreement with Le Corbusier and Gropius, but over the design of buildings there raged considerable arguments. Häring demanded that buildings too should be utilitarian and expressive of nothing but their functions and the materials employed. He found in Le Corbusier only a new kind of aesthetic manifestation. He objected to the surfaces of the 'white architecture' as not being responsive to materials, and to its forms as being determined by aesthetic and geometrical disciplines rather than by functional necessity. He considered that form should be allowed to grow in response to function rather than being imposed through geometry:

In nature, form is the result of the organisation of many distinct parts in space in such a way that life can unfold, fulfilling all its effects both in terms of the single part and in terms

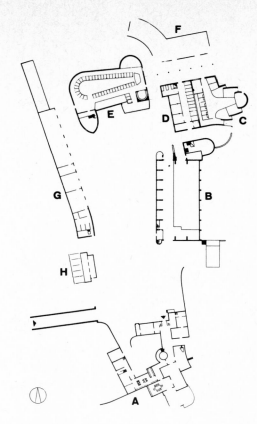

Hugo Häring. Garkau farm, Holstein, 1924, site plan; a, farmhouse; b, barn; c, pigsty; d, stable; e, cowshed; f, manure heap; g, machine sheds; h, hen house. Only b, e and g were actually constructed. Credit: Karl Krämer Verlag.

of the integrated whole; whereas in the geometrical cultures, form is derived from the laws of geometry ...

In nature all forms including crystals and other geometrically shaped ones are generated by specific internal forces, whereas in geometrical planning form is imposed from the outside, which is in opposition to its creation from within ... We must discover things and let them unfold their own forms. It goes against the grain to impose forms, to determine them from outside, to force them according to abstract laws. Basic geometrical figures are not original natural shapes for forms, they are abstract and derived from intellectual laws. The kind of unity which we construct on the basis of geometrical figures is for so many things merely a unity of form and not a unity with life ... To impose geometrical forms is to make them uniform and mechanical, but we do not want things to be mechanical except in the way they are made. To mechanise things is to give them a mechanical life, a dead life, but to mechanise the process by which they are made is to win life ... If we prefer to search for shapes rather than to propose them, to discover forms rather than to construct them, we are in harmony with nature and act with her rather than against her ... We must realise that the moment we reject our intellectual preconceptions and act in the way that nature acts, conciously planning in the way in which nature plans, we organise things in such a way that they develop a personality and serve life as a whole.[16]

This is essentially an argument against preconceptions in planning, but it is motivated by the idea that the expression or meaning of an object should be a part of its function. At root Häring's quarrel with Le Corbusier was concerned with the issue of whether or not function and expression should be separated. Le Corbusier was trying by means of geometry and proportion to produce beautiful buildings. Häring considered that the quest for beauty conflicted with a building's meaning and with its natural expression of its functions, with its 'essential rights'. He regarded the design process as a voyage of discovery which one should undertake as open-mindedly as possible. He sought meaning rather than abstract beauty. Things were to be expressive rather than aesthetic:

We now attempt not to allow our attitudes towards function to conflict with our needs for expression, but to keep them side by side ... We should not try to express our own individuality, but rather the individuality of things: their expression should be what they are.[17]

These are quotations from an essay of '25 entitled *Approaches to Form*. Häring had then just completed the building that is usually considered his masterpiece, the Garkau cowshed, so we can expect to find in it his theoretical ideas put into practice.

Garkau farm is situated near Lübeck in northern Germany. Häring planned a complete set of buildings including a large farmhouse but only the barn and cowshed were built to his design. The barn is a comparatively simple structure, rectangular in plan and with a roof built in the shape of a pointed arch. This form was not chosen out of affection for the Gothic as one might suspect, but because it allowed a structure which would only intrude minimally into the internal space, leaving as much of it free for storage as possible. It is what is known as a Lamella roof: a series of short timbers intersecting at an angle take up the line of pressure of the structure so that struts and ties can be altogether avoided.

The cowshed has a considerably more complex form. It is based on a comparatively simple but ingenious section in which the cows are stabled on either side of a central food distribution channel which can be supplied from a hayloft above. The loft floor slopes

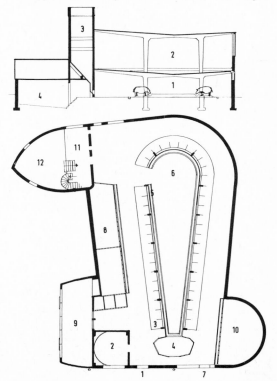

Cowshed section: 1, cowshed; 2, hayloft; 3, silo; 4, root-cellar.

Plan: 1, entrance; 2, milking parlour; 3, stalls for 41 cows; 4, stall for bull; 5, feeding trough; 6, trap from hayloft over; 7, exit; 8, heifers; 9, young bulls; 10, calves; 11, silo over; 12, root cellar.

downwards towards the centre, thus simultaneously facilitating the movements of hay towards the central delivery slot and aiding the ventilation of the cowshed below by guiding foul warm air, which of course is rising, to ventilators along the tops of the windows in the outer walls. This section, if extruded in plan, would produce a long, thin, rectangular building. So why the pear shaped layout? Partly to avoid parallel stabling of cattle which results in cows breathing on each other, spreading disease, and partly because the bull needs accommodation along with the cows, fed from the same distribution channel. He has an extra large pen at the pointed end of the plan. Here he has pride of place and seems to dominate the herd which he serves. This consideration may seem poetic rather than practical: the bull may not appreciate the architectural significance of his position. However, to have given him a stable identical with those of the cows would have seemed unsympathetic. This is a case where expression may not be altogether practically justifiable, but it is nonetheless closely related to the building's function and in no way conflicts with it.

The various adjuncts of the cowshed also have forms carefully chosen for functional reasons. The side pen for calves for example is semicircular in form to avoid

Hugo Häring. Garkau farm, Holstein, 1924. Barn interior with Lamella roof.
Barn interior with Lamella roof.

View of the farm from the approach road, cowshed on left and barn behind right, red-brown brick infill in an exposed concrete frame and green weatherboarding.

corners. In rectangular enclosures calves tend to get caught in corners when they fight and are unable to escape aggressors. The cowshed itself was constructed in a remarkably convincing mixture of ancient and modern materials: concrete frame and brick infill combined with painted timber boarding sympathetic to local tradition. Häring had an unusual sensitivity to materials and has been called a precursor of Brutalism. He is perhaps the only German architect of the twenties who never succumbed to the white render of the International Style.

The Garkau farm buildings are adventurous yet modest, progressive yet in some ways traditional. In practical terms they have been highly successful, and are visited by farmers as well as by architects. In terms of image quality they are unmistakably agricultural. Häring's aim was to lose himself in the task, to express not his own personality but the 'essence' of a cowshed.

The need to create forms constantly leads the artist to experiment with styles, repeatedly leads him, in the interest of expression, to spread shapes over objects – whereas the form arising out of work performance, the *Leistungsform*, leads to every object receiving and retaining its own essential shape. The artist stands in the most essential contradiction to the *Leistungsform* so long as he refuses to give up his individuality: for in operating with the *Leistungsform* the artist is no longer

Cowshed seen across farmyard.

concerned with the expression of his own individuality but with the expression of the essence of the most perfect possible utilitarian object.[18]

One can argue that since the architect always has to make value judgements, he is always bound to express himself. However, if he relates all his value judgements to the task in hand rather than to his own whims, responding to the situation he is building for in every way possible, his personal expression should not conflict with the expression of the building. In Häring's philosophy the architect is not a god-like dictator who imposes his will on the situation and creates out of nothing the perfect jewel, he is rather the interpreter of a building's circumstances. He helps it to be born, bringing together all the various complex forces that demand its existence.

Barn end.

Life is not given to the work by fashioning the object, the building, according to a viewpoint alien to it, but by awakening, fostering and cultivating the essential form enclosed within it.[19]

The 'essential form' is not obvious or easy to define – if it was Häring would have had many more disciples. It depends on a deeply intuitive interpretation of the architect's task, an interpretation that is bound to be subjective. Both Scharoun and Häring accepted that the architectural task could not be a totally rational process and that it necessarily depended on subjective judgements. However, they insisted that these subjective judgements should be related to the project in hand rather than to the whim of the individual or to ideas about abstract aesthetics, and this is where they stand apart from the rest of their generation.

I do not intend to spend any more time trying to define the 'essential form': it varies so much according to circumstances. The buildings and projects of Scharoun as described in Part 1 give a clearer indication of what it means than anything more I can write.

Chapter 8: The Historical Background of 'New Building'

Scharoun and Häring appear quite isolated in their divergence from the mainstream of modern architecture and historians have regarded 'new building' as a curious and interesting but historically insignificant cul de sac. It can be seen though, as an extension of an important architectural attitude that reaches back into the nineteenth century and beyond.

Häring called his philosophy 'new building' in conscious reaction against his idea of 'Architecture'. He saw an essential difference between the search for order and perfection on the one hand, which seemed to dominate classical and Renaissance architecture,

and the loose responsiveness and anonymity of medieval and vernacular building on the other. He studied medieval building closely and its influence pervades his work. It is most obvious in a house built in 1916, which has an irregular plan with an octagonal tower at one end and gothic vaulting in the entrance hall. The gothic arch form turns up repeatedly in his work, sometimes in section, sometimes in plan. In some cases it is employed for good reasons, such as in the Garkau barn, in others it seems more of a stylistic affectation. The house which he designed for Garkau farm has no superficial medieval traits but it is planned around a courtyard with a circular stair at one corner, an arrangement commonly found in large medieval houses.

Medievalism in Scharoun's work is not quite so obvious but it is there nonetheless. He created in many of his buildings a sense of progressive enclosure which parallels that of medieval buildings. This is particularly evident in the first school project, the primary school for Darmstadt of '51, and the names which Scharoun gave to parts of the complex, 'gatehouse tower' or 'meeting cloister', add to its association with things medieval. Internal courtyards are a recurrent feature in his work, one particularly striking example is a project for a church in Wolfsburg of '66, which

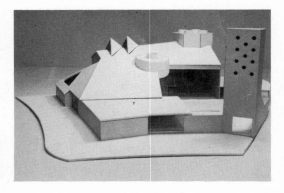

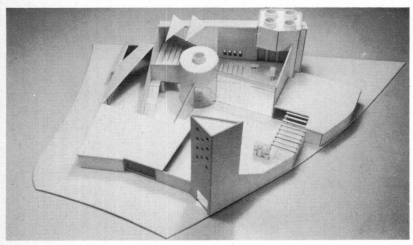

was consciously inspired by a medieval manor house plan. In this design the site is surrounded by a wall and the church, vestry, parish youth club, etc., all look into the enclosed courtyard. Medieval associations are suggested too by Scharoun's building for the architectural faculty of Berlin Technical University, also of '66. The building suggests a courtyard by enclosing a space on three sides, and has been made very hard on the convex side which is covered with grey stone cladding and separated from the pavement by an 'area' which lets light into the basement. The concave side, however, is almost entirely glazed and the semi-

Architectural Faculty, Berlin
Technical University, 1966; view
of basement garden and entrance
bridge.

enclosed space is dug out to basement level, so the building is entered by means of a bridge, an arrangement suggestive of moat and drawbridge.

Scharoun's and Häring's interest in medieval building paralleled that of the Gothic Revivalists and there are, as one might expect, links between 'new building' and Gothic Revival theory. The Gothic Revival in Germany is usually considered to have started with Goethe who, as a young man, wrote a eulogistic essay on Strasbourg Cathedral extolling the virtue of Gothic and claiming it as the authentic German architecture as opposed to the imported Renaissance which had taken over. Goethe was wrong about Gothic being essentially German, for it was later proved to have started in France, but the polemic that he had suggested remained and grew ever more popular. Gothic was seen as being Nordic in character while classicism and the Renaissance were seen as being Latin. We find this idea strongly represented in our own Gothic Revival by the writings of Pugin and Ruskin, Pugin saw the Renaissance as a cultural intrusion and attacked both Neo-Classicism and Renaissance architecture in Britain as being both inappropriate to our climate and expressive of things pagan rather than Christian. Ruskin put up similar arguments and suggested, somewhat poetically, that it was climatic differences between the Latin and Nordic

cultures that produced the differing architectural forms:

Gothic ornament stands out in prickly independence and frosty fortitude, jutting into crockets and freezing into pinnacles; here starting up into a monster, there germinating into a blossom anon knitting itself into a branch, alternately thorny, bossy and bristly or writhed into every form of nervous entanglement . . . The tribes of the north, quickened by

The hard protective exterior.

the coldness of the climate, give an expression of sharp energy to everything they do – as opposed to the languor of the southern tribes ... There is also the habit of finding enjoyment in the signs of cold which is never found, I believe, in the inhabitants of countries south of the Alps ... Instead of seeking, like the southern sculpture, to express only the softness of leafage nourished in all tenderness, and tempted into luxuriance by warm winds and glowing rays, we find pleasure in dwelling on the crabbed, perverse and morose animation of plants that have known little kindness from earth or heaven ... The work of an imagination as wild and wayward as the Northern Sea; creatures of ungainly shape and rigid limb, but full of wolfish life, fierce as the winds that beat and changeful as the clouds that shade them.[20]

Both Scharoun and Häring subscribed to the Nordic versus Latin polemic, seeing themselves as a continuation of the Nordic tradition and Le Corbusier as a continuation of the Latin. I have quoted Ruskin at some length because in his words the polemic still has a lot of appeal. Some of his statements about the perversity, awkwardness and angularity of Gothic might almost be re-applied to the work of Scharoun.

Before I get involved in what Pugin and Ruskin considered to be the difference between Nordic and Latin tradition, for them the difference between Gothic and Classical, I must give you a clearer idea of what Häring thought he was opposing. We have seen what he objected to in Le Corbusier, but Le Corbusier was for him just the tip of the iceberg, just the latest exponent of the Latin tradition, the tradition of 'Architecture' and of 'Geometry'. When he refers to 'Geometry' Häring means geometrical aesthetics, the pursuit of pure forms, proportions, etc. He does not mean just anything that can be contrived with a set square.

Geometry brings forth the idea of Architecture. It endows Architecture with the spiritual grandeur of the abstract. It celebrates timeless immutable space. Architecture rejects, 'must' reject, any building material or construction containing an element of movement as contrary to the finite and absolute which is its domain. Its buildings are made of the hardest, the most enduring stone laid in layers, each layer resting on the one underneath. It avoids tension and therefore the vault, although vaulting has been known through the ages and has been made use of in utilitarian structures. Geometry reduces building techniques to static, reposing, finite structures. This has been a conscious limitation.[21]

Häring's view of 'Architecture' is basically in agreement with that of Conrad Fiedler, a 19th century German theorist who was in the opposite camp – that is, he supported the Classical tradition:

the artistic process of creation in architecture is characterised by an alteration of form whereby materials and constructions continue to recede, while the form, which belongs to the intellect, continues to develop towards an increasingly independent existence.[22]

According to Fiedler, the essential stuff of architecture is what remains when functional, structural and practical considerations have been removed! This goes back to a particular interpretation of the origins of the Greek temple. Theorists had noted that its construction was not inherently a stone construction and that it is not efficient structurally in the way that a Gothic cathedral is. They concluded that the form of the temple had been constructed at first in timber and then later in stone, thus the magic lies essentially in the form itself regardless of the material used. Fiedler considered that because the Gothic cathedral exemplified a better use of stone than the Greek temple Gothic was inferior to Classical for, in the case of the Gothic cathedral, a potentially pure form has been polluted by structural requirements and therefore it no longer accurately represents an intellectual ideal. It would be entertaining to re-apply this argument in order to prove that Le Corbusier's Villa Savoye is better 'Architecture' than Häring's cowshed, as the pure white geometrical form of the Villa comes closer to a timeless intellectual ideal independent of material considerations than does the impure form of the cowshed, which is specific to time, place, functions and materials.

I quoted Fiedler partly to show the theoretical tradition which Häring grew up into, and partly to show how well he understood the position that he opposed. He admitted its status by allowing it the title of 'Architecture', and though he fought against Le Corbusier he had a considerable respect for him. At the end of *Approaches to Form*, Häring concluded his argument with 'we are therefore against the principles of Le Corbusier, but not against Corbusier himself'.

Between Fiedler and Häring there is another German theorist of considerable importance, Worringer. Worringer produced an important book on the Gothic around 1910 which Häring must have been aware of. In the following passage he gives the argument which Fiedler was concerned with a new twist:

Greek architecture is applied construction: Gothic architecture is pure construction. The constructive element in the first case is merely the means to a practical end; in the later case it is an end in itself, for it coincides with artistic intentions of expression.[23]

If this seems to ring of Häring, it is because Worringer was one of Häring's sources.

While these esoteric arguments were raging in Germany, rather more down to earth architectural arguments were taking place in England which indirectly had quite a strong influence on Häring. Augustus Welby Pugin has already been mentioned: he was the leader of the English Gothic Revival and was arguably the most influential English theorist of the nineteenth century. With two short books, *Contrasts* and *The True Principles of Christian or Pointed Architecture*, he changed the level of architectural thinking in England in two ways. Firstly he demanded an emphasis on design methodology and the use of materials rather than on the visual vocabulary of applied style. Secondly he emphasised that buildings had a social and cultural meaning, and that an architectural style reflected the nature of the culture that produced it. At the beginning of *The True Principles* he sets down the 'two great rules for design' as follows:

Firstly, there should be no features about a building which are not necessary for convenience, construction or propriety ... (What I mean by propriety is this, that the external and internal appearance of an edifice should be illustrative of and in accordance with, the purpose for which it is destined).
   Secondly, all ornament should consist of enrichment of the essential construction of the building.[24]

This is essentially a functionalist programme, and Pugin devotes the rest of his text to an attempt at proving that Gothic fulfills it while Classicism and the Picturesque do not. Through numerous examples he shows how Gothic structure and construction are based on sound practical reasoning with the parts visibly expressed, and materials are used with respect for their varying natures, whereas in Classicism construction is often concealed or misrepresented. Under the heading of 'propriety' he emphasises how the parts of Gothic buildings were articulated in accordance with their particular functions so that their purposes could be read in their external forms. He shows how, in 'English Catholic colleges' for instance, there is a hierarchy of articulated parts. He supplies an illustration of Magdalen College, Oxford.

The main feature of these buildings was the chapel ... The place set aside for this holy purpose generally towered over the surrounding buildings. After this principal feature, every portion of these edifices had its distinguishing character and elevation; in order to give due effect to the gate-house, refectory and other important parts of the building, the chambers never exceed the height of one storey above the ground floor.[25]

He goes on to explain why the chimneys project from the walls in the outside elevations, for 'excellent practical reasons'. Pugin then contrasts the 'ancient Catholic colleges' with 'modern collegiate buildings', showing us a simple bland symmetrical façade with evenly spaced windows. He notes how the parts are not articulated at all, but

dissolved into one uniform mass, unbroken either in outline or in face, undistinguishable from other buildings that sur-

Pugin's perspective drawing of Magdalen College, Oxford, printed in his *True Principles*.

round it. As for purpose it might be taken for a barrack hospital or an asylum.'

Formal articulation strictly related to function is of course one of the main features of 'new building' and Pugin's argument can be reapplied in its essentials, exchanging one of Scharoun's schools for the 'English Catholic colleges' and any modern rectangular school in a single envelope for 'modern collegiate buildings'.
   Formal articulation as recommended by Pugin does not allow classical planning arrangements with strict symmetries, and he ridiculed his classical opponents for forcing their buildings into symmetrical envelopes:

The classicist must have two of everything, one on each side; no matter if all the required accommodation is contained in one half of the design, a shell of another half must be built to keep up uniformity. What can be more absurd? Because a man has a real door to enter his house by on one side, he must have a mock one through which he cannot pass on the other ...

Pugin's drawing of a 'modern collegiate building' to be contrasted with Magdalen College.

All these inconsistencies have risen from this great error – the plans of buildings are designed to suit the elevation, instead of the elevation being subservient to the plan.[26]

John Ruskin borrowed from Pugin and reinterpreted his ideas in his own inimitable style. He expresses better than Pugin the responsiveness of Gothic, which is due largely to its disregard of aesthetic disciplines. Again there is a great emphasis on fitness for purpose:

The variety of the Gothic schools results not from mere love of change but from practical necessities. For in one point of view Gothic is not only the best but the *only rational* architecture, as being that which can fit itself most easily to all services, vulgar or noble. Undefined in its slope of roof, height of shaft, breadth of arch, or disposition of ground plan, it can shrink into a turret, expand into a hall, coil into a staircase or spring into a spire, with undegraded grace and unexhausted energy; and whenever it finds occasion for change in its form or purpose, it submits to it without the slightest sense of loss either to its unity or majesty – subtle and flexible like a fiery serpent, but ever attentive to the voice of its charmer. And it is one of the virtues of the Gothic builders, that they never suffered ideas of outside symmetries and consistencies to interfere with the real use and value of what they did. If they wanted a window, they opened one; a room, they added one; a buttress, they built one; utterly regardless of any established conventionalities of external appearance, knowing (as indeed always happened) that such daring interruptions of the formal plan would rather give additional interest to its symmetry than injure it. So that in the best times of Gothic, a useless window would rather have been opened in an unexpected place for the sake of surprise, than a useful one forbidden for the sake of symmetry.[27]

Ruskin goes so far in his insistence that Gothic is necessarily irregular that he claims:

If one part always answers accurately to another part, it is sure to be a bad building; and the greater or more conspicuous are the irregularities, the greater the chances that it is a good one.[28]

He then goes on to make an aesthetic virtue of complexity and irregularity, attacking simplicity and purity:

No architecture can be truly noble that is not imperfect. No human face is exactly the same in its lines on each side, no leaf perfect in its lobes, no branch in its symmetry. All admit irregularity as they imply change; and to banish imperfection is to destroy expression, to check exertion, to paralyse vitality ... No architecture is so haughty as that which is simple; which refuses to address the eye except for a few clear and forceful lines; which implies, in offering so little to our regards, that all it has offered is perfect; and disdains, either by the complexity or attractiveness of its features, to embarrass our investigation or betray us into delight.[29]

Ruskin also acknowledges, and attacks:

that love of order which makes us desire that our house windows should pair like our carriage horses, and allows us to yield our faith unhesitatingly to architectural theories which fix a form for everything and forbid variation from it.[30]

I need scarcely underline the parallels between Pugin and Ruskin's rejection of strict order, symmetry, simplicity and perfection, and Häring's rejection of 'Geometry'. We have seen how Pugin supported a strict formal articulation based on function that parallels the strict formal articulation in the work of Scharoun. We have seen too that Ruskin, Pugin, Scharoun and Häring all subscribed to the Nordic versus Latin idea, and all looked very carefully at medieval buildings. One can only conclude that 'new building' has a foot in the Gothic Revival. Did Häring and Scharoun arrive at their conclusions independently of Pugin and Ruskin, or did the English ideas percolate into Germany? Ruskin was very well known and must have been available in translation, but Pugin's influence spread to Germany largely via the Arts and Crafts movement.

Pugin was more effective as a theorist than as an architect because, although he built a surprising amount, mainly churches, all his buildings were paralysed by a painstaking fidelity to 14th-century Gothic. Largely for religious reasons he wanted to recreate a 14th-century society which, of course, proved impossible. He died a broken man, convinced that he had failed in his purpose and that his work had been in vain. He was either unable to see or unwilling to acknowledge the massive impact that his ideas were beginning to make.

Several younger architects took the *True Principles* very seriously and began to produce buildings in response to function and materials rather than applied style. Those who were less keen than Pugin on the idea of returning to the fourteenth century realised that the materials readily and economically available for building were not the same as those used in the fourteenth century. Stone was replaced to a large extent by brick, which was cheaper. Iron had become available for structural work, and glass had become more economical. Some of Pugin's followers recognised that the *True Principles* could and should be applied to the available vocabulary of construction, and they took up Pugin's functionalism without his insistence on strict fidelity to the Gothic. This approach resulted in some of the best and most original buildings put up during the Victorian era, one of which is the Red House at Bexleyheath built for William Morris by Philip Webb in 1860. This house has quite wrongly been seen by some critics as 'picturesque' when in fact it follows the *True Principles* particularly faithfully. Its red brick façades were left plain and devoid of ornament, which must have been shocking at the time, and the nature of brick construction was expressed wherever possible. Doors and windows are topped by pointed arches, and sometimes these are reinforced by restraining arches in the walls above. In the interior timber work is left plain and uncovered. Doors are of a simple and obvious construction and the wooden lintels above them purposely left bare and protruding from the wall surface. Roof structure is exposed in the ceilings of the first floor rooms and fireplaces are of exposed brickwork.

In the planning of the house the rooms were considered separately, each having a particular size, shape and distribution of windows according to its chosen function. No two rooms are the same. The different parts are expressed externally as a result of this 'planning from the inside outwards', both in the overall shape of the building and in the irregular window pattern. There is a story, possibly apocryphal but certainly characteristic, that Webb began his design by standing on the site and selecting positions for the

rooms according to view and orientation. The servants' end of the house is articulated in the overall form and treated in keeping with Pugin's statement that 'every person should be lodged as becomes his station and dignity'. The servants' stair is narrower than the main stair and the servants' bedrooms are small and plain with dormer windows set in the roof too high to allow a view out although plenty of light comes in. We may frown on the politics of this and wonder about its compatibility with the socialism of Morris and Webb, nevertheless it demonstrates an accurate response to architectural propriety.

I have given this extensive description of the Red House because it was an important prototype and is similar in its design methodology to some of the work of Häring and Scharoun. Although it has often been quoted by critics as an early example of honestly used materials, its planning has usually been ignored. It has

Philip Webb. The Red House, Bexleyheath, Kent, built for William Morris, 1860.

been called 'picturesque' I suppose because it is pervaded by a sense of romantic medievalism, but it would certainly not rate as 'picturesque' in Pugin's terms,* for its planning is all carefully reasoned and considered – there is nothing false or arbitrary. Even the well in the garden, which looks very picturesque, was in fact the source of water for the house when it was built.

Webb was Morris' right hand man and he produced designs for stained glass and furniture for the Morris firm. His architectural output consists almost entirely of country houses, built always with loving care for construction and detail, and always in close response to the chosen site and locality. The Red House marked the start of a new phase in the history of English domestic architecture. Webb had a number of contemporaries who thought along similar lines, and soon there was a profusion of irregular, asymmetrical country houses based on vernacular tradition and adapted Gothic Revival theory.

The history of this period in English domestic architecture is characterised by what Lethaby, Webb's pupil and biographer and an excellent architect in his own right, called 'sound expressive building' as opposed to 'Architecture', which he sarcastically referred to as 'that wonderful occult essence which is laid on to each of us in a private tap'. Lethaby and his contemporary Voysey soldiered on until the twenties, but they had no real followers and as a movement 'sound expressive building' died in England before the first decade of the century was out. It has been ignored as an historical phenomenon ever since. The buildings of Webb and Voysey appear in books on modern architecture as the works of early pioneers, although Voysey disowned the modern movement. Nobody looks at their works per se and nobody seems to want to read Lethaby, the best apologist for the period, for now most if not all of his writings are out of print, even his biography of Webb, the only one so far written.

As 'sound expressive building' was dying in England it was exported to the Continent largely through the efforts of one man, Hermann Muthesius. Muthesius came to England in 1896 as a cultural attaché to the German embassy in London. He made a detailed study of English domestic architecture which resulted

in a three volume history entitled *Das Englische Haus*. In the first volume he investigates house types from the 14th century onwards, in order to show changing ideas about planning and organisation, but the greater part of the text is given up to an examination of houses by Webb, Lethaby, Shaw, Nesfield, Voysey, Mackintosh, Lutyens and some other less well known Victorian architects. The second and third volumes contain extensive information about internal and external detailing, garden layout and even diagrams of hot water systems. Muthesius's study was thorough and Lethaby had later grudgingly to admit that Muthesius had indeed mastered his subject. Even now *Das Englische Haus* has not been translated and has no English counterpart. Many of the buildings described in it remain relatively unknown.

Muthesius succeeded in transplanting the dying flower of the Arts and Crafts movement, and with it many aspects of 'sound expressive building', to Germany, where it found fertile ground. In the first fifteen years of the century many German architects built houses obviously modelled on English examples. Until then German houses had been strict, formal and symmetrical but they now became free and irregular like their English forerunners. Muthesius had not been slow to point out the contrast between the two approaches:

In the English house one would look in vain for the kind of pomposity, for Style written with a capital S (or Architecture with a capital A) which we, in Germany, are still devoted to. It is already forty years since the movement against the imitation of styles began in England. It has been inspired by simple buildings in the country; and in its course, it has already yielded splendid results. Let us learn from it. The same reasonable, straightforward attitude which informs the shape of the house can be seen in the way the house is placed on the ground fitting into the surrounding countryside. It adapts itself to nature, and house and garden are treated as one closely integrated unit.[32]

Muthesius, like the Gothic Revivalists, subscribed to the Nordic versus Latin polemic:

In the art of building of the North, a window is very different in kind from what it is in Italian architecture. The art of Italy has treated it as merely a hole in the wall. The window holes are evenly distributed over the façade. Their hole-character is enhanced by their architectural frame, and the symmetry of the whole composition requires niches even in places where windows are not required. How different in Northern building! Windows are bracketed together, they appear on the outside exactly in the place where they are required within; therefore they express the interior, they reflect the very essence of the house.[33]

Muthesius was a very important figure in German architecture in the early years of the century. He was

---

*When architects avoid the defect of regularity (the classical approach) they frequently fall into one equally great with regard to irregularity; I mean when a building is *designed to be picturesque*, by sticking as many ins and outs, ups and downs, about it as possible. The picturesque effect of the ancient buildings results from the ingenious methods by which the old builders overcame local and constructive difficulties. An edifice which is arranged with the principal view of looking picturesque is sure to resemble an artificial waterfall or a made-up rock which are generally so unnaturally natural as to appear ridiculous.[31]

the leading figure of the famous Deutscher Werkbund, an organisation which owed a lot to the English Arts and Crafts movement. Everyone knew about 'The Muthesius Case', and Häring was at an impressionable age when Muthesius was at the height of his powers. When *Das Englische Haus* was published in 1904 Häring was twenty-two.

The extreme irregularities of some of the houses described by Muthesius, particularly those of Webb and Lethaby, the Germans found hard to accept. When Muthesius himself had to design a country house he chose as a model the most classical of all his examples, the symmetrical house of Edward Prior. Although around 1905 even a follower of Schinkel like Peter Behrens could produce a house influenced by the English tradition, German neo-classicism gradually reasserted itself and the whole issue of responsive irregularity was left to Häring to resurrect.

Muthesius became more and more interested in one particular aspect of the Arts and Crafts creed, the production of plain, honest furniture and utensils. He diverged from Morris in his acceptance of the machine and he championed standardisation as both necessary and desirable. He felt that only through standardisation could 'universal good taste' be established. This part of his creed passed on to Gropius and the Bauhaus. It was the part that Häring could not accept. His view of finding the essential nature of the object was basically anti-aesthetic – the object had rights of its own beyond considerations of taste.

Muthesius was opposed in his attitude to standardisation by Henri van de Velde, and in 1914 the Werkbund was almost split by their confrontation. Like Muthesius, van de Velde was very keen on the English Arts and Crafts movement and his 'credo' of 1906 could almost have been written by Pugin. He advocates that the form and construction of all objects should only be understood within the terms of the 'strictest elementary logic and justification for their existence', and that forms and constructions should be 'subordinated to the essential use of the material'. Ornament should only be applied while one can 'respect and retain the rights and essential appearance of these forms and constructions'. Van de Velde was also an exponent of Art Nouveau and he subscribed to the tradition of 'organic' architecture.[34] He may well have had some influence on Häring.

His disagreement with Muthesius was due to a belief in the sanctity of the artist; he saw standardisation as a threat to the artist's individuality. Häring would not have accepted his position any more than that of Muthesius because of its élitism, because van de Velde stood for self-expression rather than for the expression of what is being made. Häring's disagreement with both sides pinpoints the real kernel of the theory of 'new building', the part of its ethic which differentiates it from other theories. Häring avoided both of the major pitfalls that most modern architects have fallen into: prescribed taste based on supposedly universal standards, and the prescribed taste of the lone inviolable artist.

We should not express our own individuality, but rather the individuality of things: their expression should be what they are.[35]

I shall pick up this theme again in the final chapter of this book, which will be devoted to an assessment of the validity of 'new building' as represented by Scharoun's built work. For the time being we must return to the biographical coverage, to Scharoun in Berlin at the end of the Second World War.

Chapter 9: The Postwar Period

Hans Scharoun in 1946.

The 1946 Planungskollectiv plan for the re-structuring of Berlin.

After the war Scharoun was remembered by the authorities as possibly the most eminent architect available and was appointed Berlin city planning officer, the post that Martin Wagner had held in the late twenties, even before he had time to offer his services to the corporation. He immediately set about organising the reconstruction of parts of the gutted city and saved many damaged but historically valuable buildings from total demolition. The acute need for a master plan soon became obvious, but the allies had forbidden the German authorities to produce one. He therefore set up a planning group, the *Planungskollectiv*, on his own initiative, and they produced a radical reconstruction plan which was put on exhibition in '46 in the white hall of the Berlin *Schloss*, the old palace of the Kaisers which was later destroyed by the East German authorities. At that time the city was divided into four sectors by the allies for administrative purposes, but there was no major east–west split and Berliners had reason to believe that their city would eventually be returned to them intact, so for the purposes of the plan Berlin was seen as a single unit.

Before the war the old city had a tight and congested centre, sited on the original medieval development and perpetuated by a converging spider's web road pattern. Now that a substantial portion of the city had been destroyed it was possible to think of changing this basic structure. The *Planungskollectiv* proposed that the centre should be replaced by a linear development in three bands, a *Bandstadt*. The centre band was to contain official, commercial and entertainment functions, the two outer bands being taken up by residential developments. With this arrangement the commercial centre would be spread out, but a part of it would always be within easy reach of any residential quarter. The road system applied to this linear plan was a loose grid which gradually turned into a ring-radial system as it moved away from the central area. In the outer parts of the city industrial and residential developments were to have been broken up and mixed at a smaller scale than had hitherto been the case, thus promoting variety and reducing home to work travel distances.

These bold proposals were never put into practice. For political reasons, Scharoun lost his post as city planning officer within two years and his successor was very conservative, the plan he adopted being conventional and academic. In any case Berlin was destined to become a divided city. In '48 conflicts between the eastern and western powers resulted in the start of the gradual partitioning of the city which eventually culminated in the building of the notorious Wall.

In '46 Scharoun helped to re-establish the architectural faculty of Berlin Technical University and was awarded a senior professorship in the town planning department which he was to hold until '58. Between '47 and '51 he was also the head of the Institute for Building Studies at the German Academy of Sciences. With his planning and teaching duties, Scharoun was kept busy through the lean years following the war when building was severely restricted by a crippled economy. He produced only a handful of architectural projects in the late forties, and the only two projects which were actually built were conversions of Amerika Haus in Bremerhaven and of a building for the Academy at

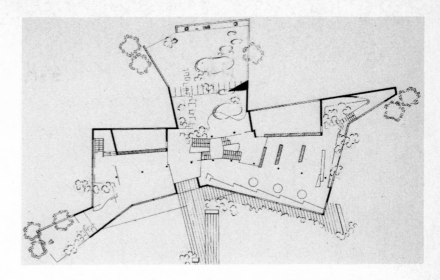

which he was teaching. Of the unbuilt projects produced at this time two in particular deserve mention here: a design for a small art gallery in Berlin and a design for a housing scheme at Berlin Friedrichshain.

The gallery project was designed for the book and art dealer Gerd Rosen in '48. It was one of the first non-residential buildings that Scharoun had worked on since the early thirties, and it provided him with one of his first opportunities to make freer use of the ideas that had emerged in the planning of the Schminke house about the use of contrasted axes. A small exhibition gallery is not the kind of project where a pressing need suggests an obvious solution since its functions are not that specifically definable. So there were probably not many clues in Scharoun's brief to suggest a definite form, and one would have expected him to have had difficulty in 'growing' a form out of the problem, as his philosophy required, rather than imposing a geometrical form as most other architects would have done. To add to his difficulties the site was flat and open so the form of the building could not convincingly have been generated by external pressures. Nevertheless he was able to discover and grow a solution out of the requirements and, although his conception cannot be regarded as functionally inevitable, it is functionally relevant.

The building has two storeys. On the ground floor are the book section, information desk and manager's office; on the first floor are the rooflit picture gallery and one small book gallery. The central staircase linking these two floors is the key to the over-all form of the building and was the starting-point of the plan. The outer walls follow the angles of this staircase and the gallery spaces seem to have been thrown outwards from it. The staircase itself is double, with a shared landing, and permits four different routes from floor to floor. Such over-rich circulation elements are a favourite device of Scharoun. They flatter the user with a choice of direction, giving him a strange sense of freedom and an impression of spatial fluidity. Where the two upper flights of the stair arrive at the first floor each faces a screen, and the visitor would be forced to move either to the right or to the left. This abrupt punctuation of the circulation course seems quite opposed to the smooth flowing continuity which we have seen in the later foyers for theatres and concert halls, where routes are direct and obvious and angle changes are carefully softened. But in the gallery the function of the stairs is different: they are less important in terms of practical circulation but more important in terms of visual and spatial experience. They are not likely to be heavily used and there is no danger

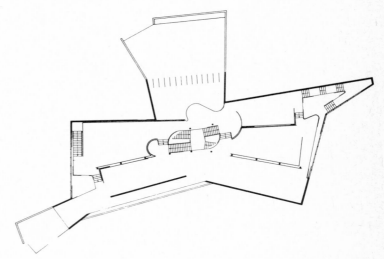

of congestion. The screen is placed in front of each stair to prevent the whole space beyond being visible at once: without it the upper galleries would reveal all their secrets to the visitor before he had reached the top of the stair.

To read the plan of the gallery sympathetically one must forget about its quality as an abstract shape or as a visual composition on paper and, instead, take an imaginary walk around it, paying careful attention to what at every point Scharoun is encouraging one to

Gerd Rosen Art Gallery project, Berlin, 1948; ground floor plan.

Above
First floor plan.

Model.

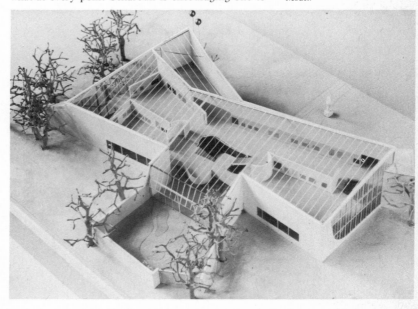

see and what he is preventing one from seeing. He has organised the varying spatial experience with supreme skill: vistas open and close, sometimes gradually, sometimes suddenly. Differences in level are used dramatically and transitions between one level and another are stressed, each time in a different way. The two side staircases between the ground and first floor, for example, are strongly contrasted: one is tightly enclosed and slips up sideways to the upper gallery revealing it quite suddenly, while the other takes you almost completely out of the building and then brings you back in up three short flights of steps separated by landings. This stair faces directly into the galleries, and so the visual experience of arriving at the upper floor is not postponed by a screen in this case but is on the contrary deliberately lengthened and exaggerated.

These effects may seem rather theatrical, but they are, arguably, appropriate to an art gallery. Some critics have suggested parallels between Scharoun's work and the Baroque because of this theatricality, and it is interesting to note that in Häring's philosophy the Baroque does belong to the tradition of the Nordic cultures and is considered an architecture of movement.

The first floor of the gallery is very enclosed along the length of the building, having windows looking out only in the end walls and over the rear sculpture court, so the predominant visual axis runs along the length of the building. However, on the ground floor the per-

pendicular axis becomes much stronger. It starts with the approach path outside, which runs towards the middle of the building into a façade made concave by the angle change originating in the staircase. This slight concavity gives the building a little control of the space in front of it and produces a hint of enclosure which a flat façade would not have done. The path changes angle before it reaches the building, the original axis being closed by a sculpture. But behind this sculpture is a window through which the main staircase would be visible, and behind that the rear sculpture court would be partly visible through another window, so visually the axis of the approach path runs right through the building at right angles to the internal circulation pattern, creating a dramatic contrast at the focal point – which is of course the main staircase, that feature in which the building discloses its beginning and its end.

This art gallery design is very revealing. It shows us what Scharoun chose to concentrate on when given a project with a loose brief. Most architects would have tried to play formal games but Scharoun played spatial games instead. There is a fundamental distinction here. One can imagine what, for example, Le Corbusier might have done with this project, pursuing his favourite practice of contrasting free and disciplined forms. He might have produced a building with fascinating spatial relationships but it would have been quite unlike Scharoun's. For in Le Corbusier's work space is always counterbalancing form, and is therefore always disciplined by form, whereas in Scharoun's buildings space is set free and form becomes subservient to it. The building envelope is considered flexible, it can be pushed in and out or punctuated at will in the planning process without answering to any formal system, and in the end it is only limited by the bounds of what can conveniently be constructed. The spatial qualities of Scharoun's buildings are fundamentally different from those of Le Corbusier's buildings and the two are irreconcilable: their different advantages cannot be combined.

At around the time the gallery was conceived, Scharoun was also working on his largest ever housing project, the planning of a neighbourhood unit beside the Stalinallee in Berlin Friedrichshain. This scheme falls chronologically between the two large developments planned by Scharoun that were actually built, Siemensstadt and North Charlottenburg, but it is much larger than either of these. It it interesting to see how he intended to cope with such a scale. He stressed in his report on the project how 'just adding flats up one on top of another is not enough', and how

Plan for housing beside the Stalinallee, Berlin Friedrichshain, 1949.

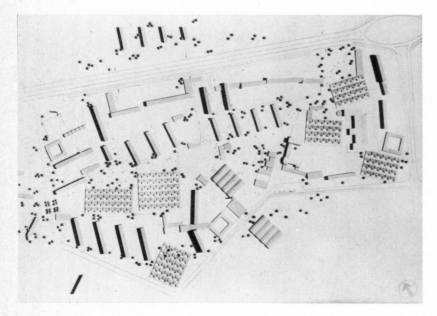

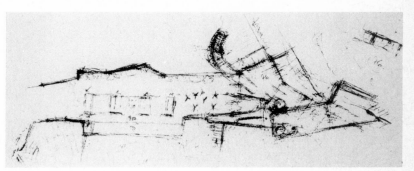

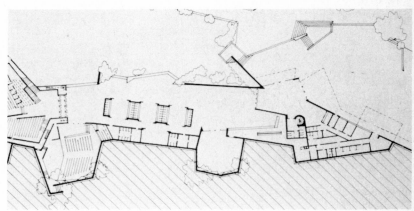

a neighbourhood must come together as a coherent organic whole to form a recognisable unit. When faced with the choice of housing type, rather than developing one supposedly ideal solution and repeating it as many architects would have done, he developed a whole range of different types, from single storey courtyard houses on the one hand to multi-storey point blocks on the other. In this way he felt he could cater for a variety of needs and tastes besides adding to the richness of the scheme. The different dwelling types are mixed up together in different combinations in different parts of the site, thus creating a profusion of open spaces varying in shape and size which would give each part a specific character and sense of place, avoiding meaningless repetition. But despite this apparently undisciplined treatment the neighbourhood is conceived as a whole, its external limits being set by the surrounding roads, since only cul de sac inroads penetrate the site. The focus of the neighbourhood is an open central square where community functions are placed together. Here one would find a shopping centre, a laundry, a school, a kindergarten and an administration building.

The site on which the project was to have been built fell within the Russian sector of Berlin, and it was planned at a time when east–west relations were deteriorating, so the growing political split between the great powers soon sealed its fate, and in the end the plan was scrapped. Fortunately Scharoun was able to bring many of the ideas pioneered in the scheme to fruition later at North Charlottenburg where their worth is amply demonstrated.

In '49 Scharoun produced his first postwar competition designs: one for an opera house in Leipzig and another for a Liederhalle in Stuttgart. The latter was awarded first prize but was never built. From this time onwards competition entries took up an increasing share of his energies. Of the thirty-six listed projects between '50 and '60, nineteen were competition entries and of these nineteen no less than ten were awarded prizes, including four firsts and three seconds. Despite the successes Scharoun never made much money out of his projects. He and his wife lived very largely on his teaching salary and later on his teaching pension, and he used the money won in competitions to finance his small office. His working method was necessarily time consuming and therefore expensive.

He would spend months on the basic conception of a building at the level of sketches, drawing and redrawing, at first very roughly and later more precisely to investigate the potentialities of different formal relationships. Each project was a new voyage of discovery,

and he only found each of those neat, convincing, original solutions at the end of a prolonged search. Gradually the plan would emerge from the murky depths of the imprecise sketches, growing slowly clearer and clearer as each part gained an accurate definition. The ruler, compass and protractor with their inflexible disciplines were kept safely out of the way until the design had become definite enough to accept their services. The characteristic acute and obtuse angles in the plan were not set up with a protractor but emerged as a result of the way in which the different plan elements could best relate to one another. Thus it is no good measuring them with the protractor. They turn out generally not to be a neat 20° or 30° but 21·36° or 34·91° – without geometrical significance. In fact the angles are quite irrelevant, they never need be measured except in considering constructional details. After the sketch stage a Scharoun plan would be post-rationalised on a system of lengths and co-ordinates. The position of any point on the plan can always be accurately defined in terms of its distance from two other points whose positions are already known. Buildings are normally set out by this method of triangular co-ordination, so whether or not their corners are at 90° makes very little difference.

The gradual development of a plan through sketches – the foyer of the competition scheme for Wolfsburg theatre.

[97]

Most of the important projects done by Scharoun in the fifties and sixties have already been described in the first part of this book so I only need mention them in passing to clarify the chronological perspective. The first two major schemes of the fifties were the Darmstadt school project of '51 (p. 15) and the Kassel theatre project of '52 (p. 26). However, between these two lies a third project of some significance, a competition entry for the American Memorial Library at Berlin Kreuzberg, which was awarded second prize.

At first sight this library scheme has perhaps the most arbitrary looking plan that Scharoun ever produced but on close examination it turns out, as usual, to have been carefully assembled. The building consists essentially of two parts, a sprawling irregular ground floor containing most of the public functions and a compact, disciplined, ten storey block very largely given over to book storage. These two parts are loosely interrelated: the regular grid of columns supporting the block has not been allowed to dictate

the planning of the ground floor, but has rather become absorbed into it.

The site lay close to Mehringplatz, a famous circus which in prewar days had been one of the highspots of Berlin. Between the site and Mehringplatz run an elevated railway and a canal. Scharoun saw the ten storey block as the externally dominant feature of his building, the only part that could compete for attention with other multi-storey buildings in the area. It presented a large flat surface in elevation, like a hoarding, which could be used to carry decoration drawing attention to the library, and he placed it parallel to road and railway for maximum effect. It is shown in the elevation drawing with a sculpture representative of the patronage of the building and a series of interlocking rings which were intended, I suspect, to represent a display of fluorescent lights. An outline of the elevated railway is also imposed on this elevation to show the level at which it runs. This is in a way misleading for it suggests that the railway is much closer to the

American Memorial Library project, Berlin, 1951. Ground floor plan; 1, main entrance; 2, bicycle park; 3, information desk; 4, newspapers; 5, periodicals; 6, self-service library; 7, staff; 8, index; 9, offices; 10, lecture hall; 11, public w.c.s; 12, children's library; 13, administration.

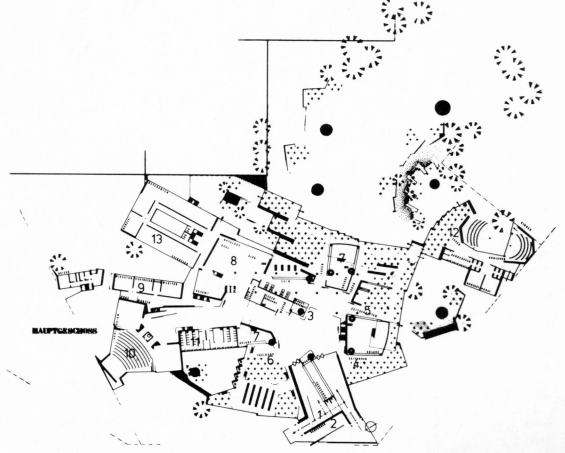

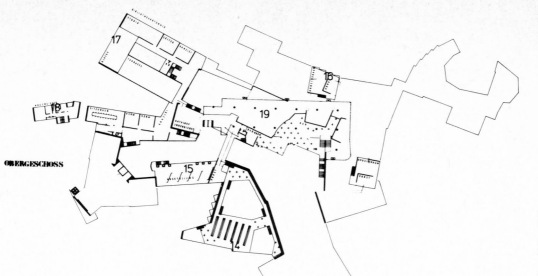

17

OBERGESCHOSS

19

18

15

14

Diagrammatic ground floor plan to clarify elements.

Centre
Elevations.

Bottom
Projection.

building than is evident from the site plan, but its inclusion in the drawing does show us the importance which Scharoun attached to the view from the train.

In the layout of the ground plan the usual formal articulation is evident. Thus the film and lecture hall, two wings of offices, a block of lavatories and a detached unit containing heating plant and caretaker's flat are all evident on the left-hand side of the plan, while the section of the building almost detached from the rest on the right is the children's library with its own entrance. In the central part of the building articulation is less obvious as the parts are more fluidly related and irregularly shaped. Five reading areas are served by librarians from five different counters: the area immediately to the left of the main entrance is the self-service library, and it has an extension on the first floor,

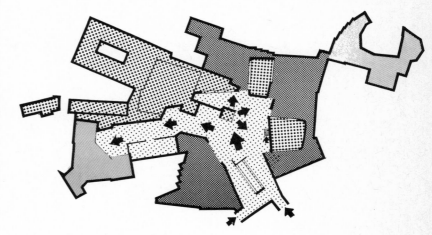

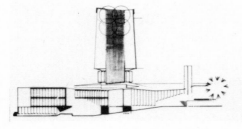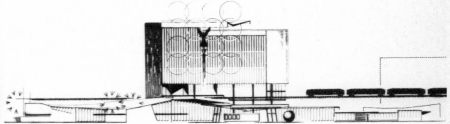

while the area to the right of the main entrance is reserved for newspapers and magazines.

In the relation of the various elements of the ground floor plan, circulation was a strong consideration. The bifurcated main entrance was placed on the street corner where it would have the most direct access across the street to Mehringplatz and to the local railway station. One entrance faces directly across the street while the other links up with a pedestrian route eastwards. Inside the building the two routes run parallel into a double-height hall towards the central information desk which acts as the hub of an essentially radial circulation system. There is also a very wide, direct circulation route linking the entrance with the film and lecture hall, taking in the lavatories on the way. This is the one route which would be expected to carry heavy pedestrian traffic and it was made wide and smooth flowing in consequence.

The planning of the library shows Scharoun at his freest. Although the plan is convincingly assembled and would have resulted in a very exciting building

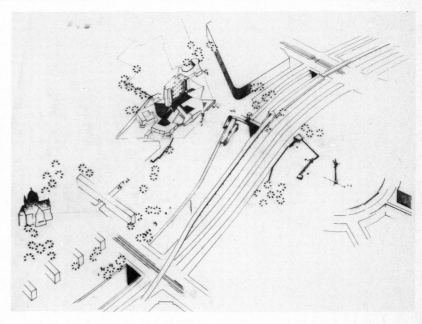

with an enormous variety of spaces and different aspects, its sheer irregularity would have given rise to numerous constructional problems. The same sort of irregularity is evident in the other major projects of that period, the Darmstadt school and the Kassel theatre, and the disappointment of losing the commission of the latter project because of presumed constructional difficulties caused Scharoun to discipline his planning rather more in later years. Thus when he came to design his second library, the state library of Berlin presently under construction, he made the various parts much more rectangular in themselves so that irregularities could be confined to the areas where major angle changes take place.

After the Kassel project came a stream of designs that have already beeen described: in '52 the prize winning old people's home (p. 55) and the commended Heligoland plan (p. 54), in '53 the Mannheim theatre project (p. 29), and in '54 the planning of the Romeo and Juliet flats (p. 48). By this time Scharoun had built up a considerable reputation and various honours were bestowed upon him, including the Fritz Schumacher prize, the Berliner Kunst prize, and a doctorate at the Technical High-school in Stuttgart. In '55 he helped to re-establish the Berlin Arts Academy and became its president. In '56 he planned the North-Charlottenburg development (p. 46) and the school at Lünen (p. 18) besides winning the competition for the Philharmonie (p. 36). With these three projects under way '57 was a blank year for new schemes, and only one new project is listed for that year, an entry for the Bremen town hall competition. In '58 came the Saarbrucken concert hall design (p. 42) and two other competition projects hitherto unmentioned: one for the replanning of central Berlin, the other for a town hall at Marl. Both projects were awarded second prizes.

The Berlin as a Capital City competition was announced by the West German authorities in '57. Architects from several countries were invited to submit schemes for the rebuilding of about four square miles of the city, an area stretching from Alexanderplatz to the Tiergarten. This had been the original centre of Berlin, but it was almost totally devastated at the end of the war and had remained largely in ruins because of its unfavourable position on the dividing line between east and west sectors of the city. The purpose of the competition was to establish a plan for this central area which could be implemented when the two halves were re-united and Berlin had become once more the capital of a unified Germany. The new centre was to accommodate all government functions and cultural elements including university, national library, museums and art gallery as well as the usual commercial and economic functions associated with city centres. There was to be no residential quarter within the central area as it was assumed that many of the areas bordering it would be residential.

Altogether 151 entries were received by the sponsors, including one by Le Corbusier and one by Mart Stam. The first prize and one of the two second prizes were awarded to German schemes of an academic and monumental character, with stiff rectangular planning and every building parcelled off neatly on its plot. Both schemes were relatively conservative and did not really break any new ground; they seem to have been selected by the jury because they were considered safe. Among the lesser prize winners were several more radical proposals concerning buildings of gigantic and unprecedented scale, and new kinds of movement organisation. Le Corbusier's entry was disappointingly predictable and it gained no award. It contained all the usual Corbusier building types, the varying types of high block, the spiral museum, etc., dotted around on green spaces which were broken up with a formal network of roads. The grandiose major avenues ran in straight lines right across the site.

Scharoun and Ebert his collaborator, a former member of the *Planungskollectiv*, had the advantage of a thorough knowledge of Berlin and its planning problems. Their entry, which took the second of the two second prizes, was widely considered to be the most sophisticated of all the proposals, and some critics thought it the only one worth taking seriously. Unlike most of the other competitors Scharoun and Ebert did not try to impose any kind of over-all monumental pattern on the city but concentrated rather on solving each problem that arose in its own particular context. They accepted the complexity of the situation and acknowledged the need for a great deal of variety in terms of scale, building type and layout treatment. Thus they were ready to accommodate the remaining historic buildings into their plan in a respectful manner and even sought to recreate some of the celebrated highspots of old Berlin. They resurrected the historic Unter den Linden, for example, with a new building layout of classical formality where government ministries would be housed, but elsewhere on the site the looser planning arrangements more usually associated with Scharoun are more in evidence.

In spite of the formal looseness of the plan it has a very definite structure and a strong over-all conception. The ring road which surrounds the area was an obligatory element dictated by the competition organisers, but the layout of routes within it was left

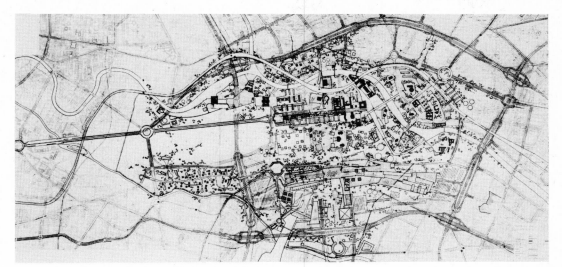

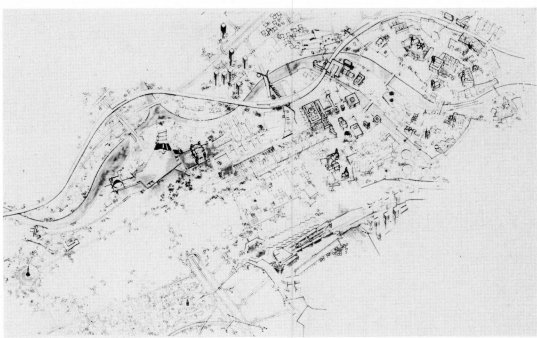

Project for the redevelopment of
Central Berlin, 1958, plan and
projection.

at the discretion of the competitors. Scharoun and Ebert decided against having any substantial through roads in the central area. They devised a system of loop roads to run parallel with parts of the ring road, providing local links and collector paths for the ring. Other roads within the site were to be organised according to the needs of the various buildings, which were distributed according to function in a layout which is essentially linear, running from east to west. This linearity is reminiscent perhaps of the Bandstadt idea in the '46 plan, but it is also sympathetic to the site as it follows the valley of the river Spree, the strongest natural feature of the locality. The project was entitled The Valley and the Hill, 'valley' referring to the river valley along which political and cultural elements were distributed, 'hill' to an immense linear building housing all commercial functions to be placed to the south of the river valley. This building, which would be about as long as London's Oxford Street, was based on a complex multilevel circulation system running

from end to end and distributed in section as follows: sub basement, commercial vehicles; basement, long-term parking; ground level, pedestrians; first floor, short-term parking; second floor, buses; third floor, pedestrians. This circulation system could be 'plugged into' anywhere along its length and at the appropriate level, according to the varying needs of the elements added, so the final envelope of the building would be dictated by the various pressures of its detailed parts, and the shape shown on the plan is only a rough indication of how it might be. In the report this open-ended approach to this part of the planning is expressed as follows:

Space must be found in the centre of the city for a large number of agencies, and for each of these agencies there is a particular solution for (a) building form, (b) traffic circulation (c) relationship to the total environment of Berlin, to be found ...[36]

This open-endedness is very important. The

[101]

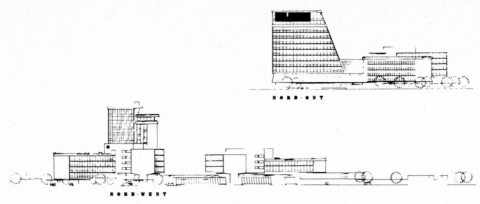

Scharoun–Ebert scheme was conceived at a much less formal level than most of the others proposed. It does not constitute a closed system based on unalterable laws but rather a pile of ideas which can be manipulated and added to. It does not demand any great overall consistency in style and building type, and could best be implemented not by one team of architects with one coherent house style, but by a large number of different architects representative of the whole spectrum of modern architectural tradition, from the most classical to the most organic. Once again it is richness and meaning that are sought rather than aesthetic consistency.

The other project of '58, the scheme for a town hall at Marl, can give us perhaps a clue as to how Scharoun might have treated his vast commercial building in Berlin had he tackled it in detail. For the Marl project is extremely large and complex with a number of different elements treated in different ways. The design formula must be familiar by now: first the elements are designed one by one specifically, and then they are put together in such a way that their identity is preserved. One advantage of this approach is that a large building becomes effectively an aggregate of small buildings, so its scale does not become overpowering, for the size of the human being is always respected.

As far as new projects were concerned '59 was another lean year for Scharoun. He was busily engaged in the detailed design of the Philharmonie and the Geschwister Scholl school at Lünen was under construction. The only new project listed for that year is a town planning scheme for Hamburg in which he was called in as expert adviser. At around that time he received two more honours in recognition of his services: the Great Federal Cross of Merit and a medallion from the Free Arts Academy at Hamburg.

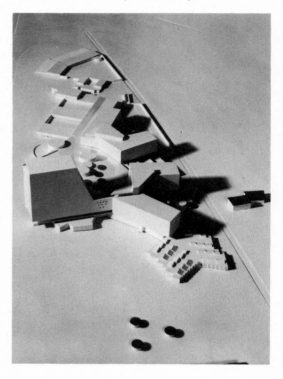

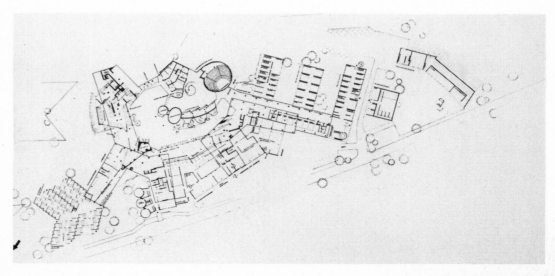

Chapter 10: The 1960s and the Last Works

In '60 the construction of the Philharmonie began on site, and its management took up a large share of Scharoun's energy until its completion in October '63. The only major new projects done within this period were the primary school at Marl of '60 (p. 23), the Salute block of flats at Stuttgart of '61 (p. 50), and a competition scheme for the rebuilding of Frankfurt's

cathedral square of '63, which was awarded third prize. The Philharmonie was opened to great public acclaim on 15 October 1963, with a concert given by the Berlin Philharmonic orchestra under Herbert von Karajan. Scharoun had finally proved himself capable of putting his most daring ideas into practice, and in subsequent years a higher proportion of his projects were actually built than ever before.

Perhaps it was the success of the Philharmonie that won him the commission for the German Embassy at Brasilia which was designed late in '63 and eventually completed in '71. This is Scharoun's only building outside Germany. The site was a rectangular plot of open ground, with a slight slope from end to end, on the southern outskirts of the new city. The accommodation required included chancellery offices, the Ambassador's residence with facilities to entertain numerous guests, and dwellings for the embassy staff. Climatic problems were obviously an important design consideration as Brasilia lies in between the equator and the Tropic of Capricorn, quite close to the latter. At this latitude it is hot all the year round and the sun is overhead twice, once shortly before and once shortly after the midsummer of the southern hemisphere. Thus for a short period the sun would shine from the south but at a very steep angle, while for the rest of the time it would shine from the north. Eastward and westward facing façades would be open to the low but intense sun of morning and evening, so the only side reasonably free from solar glare problems would be the south side.

Characteristically, Scharoun chose to tackle each

Hans Scharoun in 1962, photo credit: Wolfgang Albrecht.

German Embassy at Brasilia, 1963. Site plan; 1, Ambassador's residence; 2, Chancellery; 3, Chancellor's house; 4, steward's house; 5, chauffeur's house; 6, caretaker's house; 7, staff accommodation.

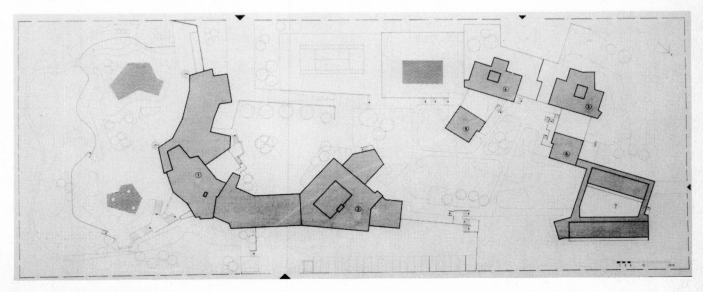

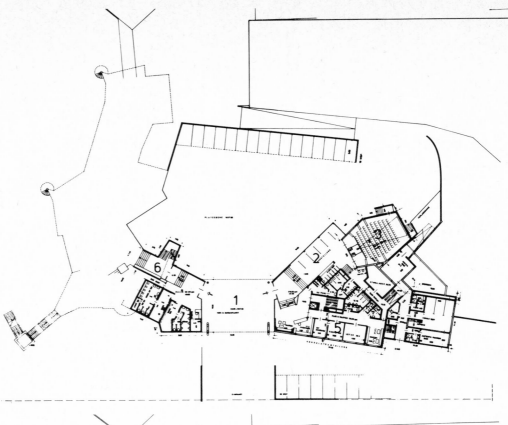

German Embassy at Brasilia, 1963. Ground and first floor plans of the main building; 1, covered entrance; 2, exhibition; 3, lecture hall; 4, w.c.s; 5, Consulate; 6, entrance to Ambassador's residence; 7, reception room; 8, music and ladies' room; 9, gentlemen's room; 10, library; 11, formal dining-room; 12, kitchen; 13, private dining-room; 14, private sitting-room; 15, Ambassador's bedroom; 16, guest bedroom; 17, children's rooms; 18, office reception; 19, offices and administration; 20, staff canteen.

N

View of Ambassador's residence.

item of accommodation required separately and to use the over-all layout of the buildings to break up the site space into specialised areas. The chancellery and Ambassador's residence make up the main building, which is basically linear in form and curls around the visitors' car park. The two parts of the building are divided by the official drive which runs through the middle of it at ground floor level with the first floor bridging the gap. This provides a shaded space where important visitors can alight from their cars. Most of the residence is orientated approximately southwards, looking out downhill across a landscaped garden away from the city. The main part of the residence is given over to a luxurious suite of rooms for entertaining,

interrelated in a very fluid manner with frequent changes in level. Beyond this region the rest of the residential wing is taken up in a series of large bedrooms, each with a private bathroom.

The chancellery is a compact four storey block containing a lecture hall, offices and conference rooms, with a central stack of services. Its approximately triangular plan shape produces a continuation of the enclosure of the parking space, allows the accommodation to converge on the main entrance, and conveniently presents one face directly southwards. Protruding from the northern end of the chancellery at first floor level is the staff canteen. Dwellings for the embassy staff are distributed around the northern end of the site. There are three detached courtyard houses, and a kind of hostel for unmarried staff which has two wings of single bedrooms enclosing a tapered courtyard and a group of communal living/dining facilities at one end.

Because of the climatic conditions strict measures of solar control were necessary and, in keeping with his general design philosophy, Scharoun welcomed these as part of the external expression of his buildings. On the chancellery block the short north-facing side, the worst from the point of view of solar heat gain, is completely blank, while the west and north-east sides are provided with deep horizontal sunbreaks, and the relatively sun-free south side has normal windows. The short south-east side has windows in the top two floors, but these are very shallow and are shielded from the sun by horizontal screens protruding from the wall above. On the residence, windows overlooking the garden on the south side are relatively large but they are protected from the high southern sun by the projection of the roof above them. This embassy project is a tribute to Scharoun's imagination, for he has once again created a strong sense of place on a site which must have looked at first very unpromising: a patch of scrubby treeless open ground fenced off unsympathetically in a strict rectangle.

One further project from '63 deserves coverage here, a competition entry for the rebuilding of Mehringplatz in Berlin. Mehringplatz has already been mentioned in connection with the American Memorial Library project of '51 (p. 98). It was a large circus at the junction of several important routes and had been one of the focal points of Berlin in prewar days, but the buildings had been flattened in the war and most of the streets had subsequently been rerouted or had lost their importance with the city divided. The competition was set up to find a new form and a new role for Mehringplatz while preserving if possible its historical

associations. Scharoun won first prize with a remarkably neat formal solution in which the circus was rebuilt as two concentric rings with a green space in the centre and a pedestrian street between the rings. The large office buildings demanded were placed outside the rings in a balanced but asymmetrical arrangement.

A diluted version of this plan is being implemented: the two rings are being built approximately as planned

German Embassy at Brasilia, 1963. Aerial photograph.

Plan for the rebuilding of Mehringplatz, Berlin, 1963.

Model below.

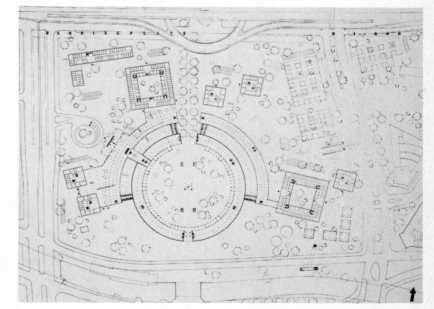

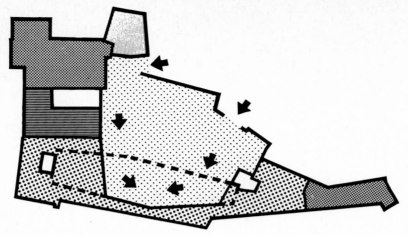

State Library, Berlin, 1964–77.
Diagrammatic plan of library to
show elements.

but cars have been admitted into part of the space between them. Scharoun was involved in the design of the first office building, that built for the AOK organisation at the south-west corner, and there is some evidence of his influence in the planning of the ground floor, but most of the building is the work of Bodo Fleischer. The grand entrance and underground car park of Scharoun's original plan were abandoned, and now most of the space outside the outer ring is given over to car parking. The inner ring is presently under construction with buildings by Werner Dütt-mann. The end result should be quite pleasant but unfortunately not as Scharoun intended it.

With both the Philharmonie and the Salute block at Stuttgart completed Scharoun was free once again in '64 to turn his attention to new projects, and in that year he produced entries for four important competitions. The first of these was the Pforzheim concert hall scheme (p. 43), the second the Zurich theatre scheme (p. 30), the third was a design for BP offices in Hamburg which gained a minor award, and the last was a design for the state library of Berlin, which was awarded first prize. This library, which is presently under construction and due for completion in '78, will be Scharoun's largest building ever and one of his most important works. It is taking ten years to build and is budgeted at over 200 million marks, which works out at around £33 million. For comparison, the Philharmonie cost 17 million marks in '63 (£2·8m) and the Mies National Gallery cost 25 million marks in '68 (£4·1m). It is being built for and financed by the Institute of Prussian Culture and will house a collection

of some 4 million books, functioning primarily as a reference library like that of our British Museum.

The library is sited at the corner of the Tiergarten, next to the Philharmonie and the Mies National Gallery, on part of the area set aside for cultural buildings quite close to the Wall, where they will be advantageously placed near the new centre if the city is ever reunited. The site area is defined by two major roads and a projected motorway and is basically triangular in shape with the most pointed end northward. Scharoun decided to place the back of the building against the motorway, making it hard and sheer, rising almost immediately to its full height of eleven storeys. This side of the building forms a sort of basic spine, containing administrative and technical facilities from end to end. The central section of it contains the cataloguing offices with a tower of six storeys containing book storage above and two more storeys of book storage in the basement, all linked together by a series of small book lifts which also serve the librarians at a variety of different levels.

In contrast with the hard motorway side, the other long side of the site faces westward into the space between the various cultural buildings and was the obvious side for main public entrances, so here the treatment is softer and more fragmentary. There are open spaces in front of the building, and it rises to its full height in three steps, starting at two storeys. The part of the library devoted to the public is placed centrally on this side. The ground floor contains the public catalogue, lending counter and a toplit exhibition space. The second floor is taken up by a vast reading room at several different levels, lit from above by a sawtooth northlight roof via circular diffusers. Linking these two main floors is a monumental double stairway system with a huge landing near the back of the building where the main information desk is placed. This stairway system develops out of the circulation axes suggested by the two main ground floor entrances, which are placed, quite logically, at opposite ends of the public part of the building.

The short south-facing end of the site is occupied by the two subsidiary institutions included in the complex, the Ibero-American Institute and a college for librarians. These are developed almost as separate units, each with its own entrance and with internal courtyards for daylighting. The main lecture hall belonging to the public part of the building protrudes almost to the site boundary on the western side, differentiating strongly between the main part of the building and the Ibero-American Institute.

The library as a whole is so large and so complex

Site plan; 1, Tiergarten; 2, Philharmonie; 3, future chamber music hall; 4, site of future museums; 5, St Mathew's Church; 6, future cultural hostel; 7, National Gallery (by Mies van der Rohe); 8, State library; 9, ring road; 10, canal.

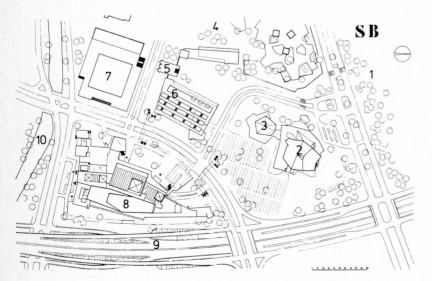

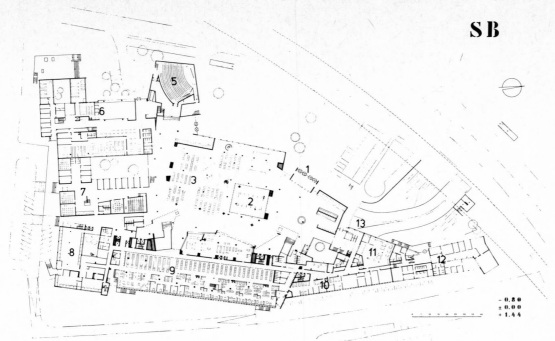

Ground floor plan; 1, main entrance; 2, book exhibition; 3, public index; 4, lending library; 5, lecture hall; 6, Ibero-American Institute; 7 school for librarians; 8, binding; 9, cataloguing and bibliography; 10, accession; 11, mail dept.; 12, Institute of Library Technology; 13, road entrance to basement parking.

that a detailed examination of the planning of its various departments would take up an inappropriately large portion of this text. The reader should by now be familiar enough with Scharoun's planning methods to make his own examination. He will find that, as usual with Scharoun, each formal differentiation reflects a functional differentiation. For instance, the various levels of the reading room reflect its division into specialist sectors.

The scale of the library is quite unprecedented. The reading room reaches a height of 9 metres and the ground floor reaches 6. This is almost the scale of a

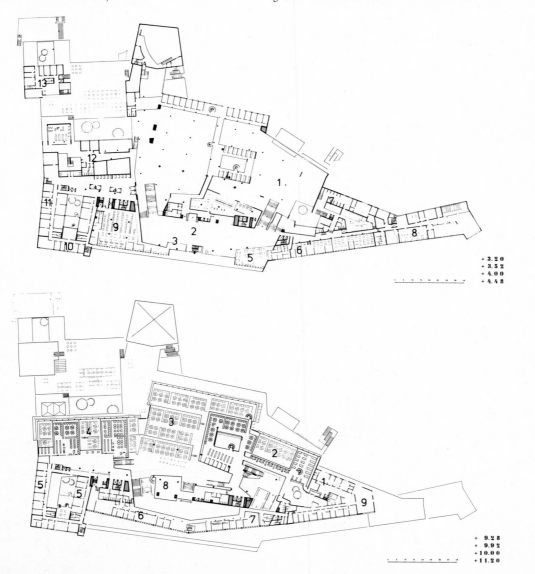

First floor plan; 1, void over ground floor; 2, 'the way of the visitor', a vast landing at the heart of the building which ties together all the main staircases; 3, main information desk; 4, private study rooms; 5, smoking room; 6, accession; 7, microfilm dept.; 8, Institute of Library Technology; 9, index of foreign literature; 10, restoration; 11, music; 12, school for librarians; 13, Ibero-American Institute.

Third floor plan; 1, general administration; 2, periodicals reading room; 3, general reading room; 4, specialist reading room; 5, specialist study rooms; 6, photo-copying; 7, documentation; 8, exhibition concerning the history of the library; 9, conference room.

railway station! Walking around the bare shell as it was in the summer of '73 was an impressive experience, but it was almost impossible to judge what the final effect would be with internal surfaces finished and furniture installed, for these things will make the scale more obvious. However, I have the feeling that Scharoun's seemingly unerring instinct for spatial values will be found to have triumphed again.

The northern wing of the building, which contains offices and the staff canteen, is already completed and in operation. The canteen is, perhaps surprisingly, provided with a sawtooth northlight roof as well as horizontal windows at eye level to provide a view out. The roof lighting may seem to some people an unnecessary extravagance, but the quality of space and light it produces is magnificent.

The exterior of the finished part is clad in grey-green granite while the interior boasts a variety of goodly finishes. No expense seems to have been spared, and constructional detailing should satisfy even purists. For a Scharoun building it seems remarkably tidy and well-behaved, but here and there one does find those playful and humorous touches which have always been a delight to some and anathema to others. One such is a window on the staircase of the north wing, which appears in the external elevation as a series of vertical slots. It turns out that a normal window has been placed behind gaps in the granite cladding. Although this curious feature was introduced primarily for fire prevention, it also allows light to enter in an interesting manner while preventing too much concentration on the view, and makes a pleasant contrast with another window at the top of the stairs which is meant to be looked out of. The latter is one of those

Section; 1, air-conditioning; 2, bookstore; 3, manuscript store (both served by multiple booklifts); 4, storage with direct access; 5, documentation; 6, the 'way of the visitor', heart of the circulation system; 7, cataloguing; 8, lending library; 9, general reading room; 10, private study rooms; 11, book exhibition; 12, general index; 13, garage; 14, heating plant; 15, book storage.

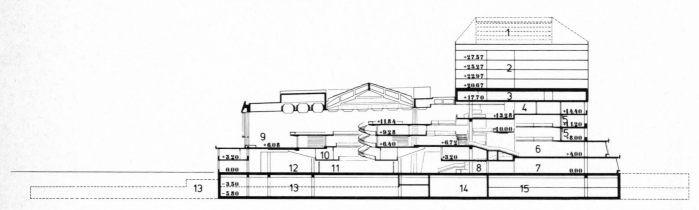

General view from north-west, taken in 1973.

circular windows which Scharoun was always so fond of, and as one walks towards the doors of the canteen it frames a view of the Philharmonie.

As has already been noted, the library faces the National Gallery building by Mies van der Rohe. Scharoun seems to have made one or two concessions to it in his design. The front of the main part of the reading room is of similar size to the visible part of the gallery and has similar fenestration. Also, inside the gallery one finds vast tapering cruciform concrete columns which seem to echo the eight cruciform steel columns supporting Mies's monumental coffered steel roof.

To assess the success or failure of the library we shall have to wait until it is finished. Some people will consider that spending £33 million on a single building

is extravagant, but this is a small figure in relation to the financial expenditure involved in some industrial developments, and mere peanuts in relation to the annual expenditure of the West German government. Always in the past, whether one is considering the Gothic cathedrals or the Victorian monuments of London, some public buildings were put up with great pride, no expense spared, as representative of the people and their age. The enjoyment gained both by the people involved at the time and by later generations, seems in general to outweigh the material cost. Scharoun had long felt the importance of such buildings, buildings which could be used, appreciated and enjoyed by all, and he had long felt the economic restrictions imposed on them. In his report for the Kassel theatre project of '52 he complained:

It is just the character of this era that industrial projects are planned generously and spaciously, and a single firm can now occupy a larger area than did a complete medieval town; whereas public projects are treated meanly and in a comparatively narrow-minded manner. Property boundaries and site dimensions always seem to restrict community buildings, but the landscape is freely used to serve technical developments, being adapted in the same way as is our society, right down to the level of the man in the street. We are greatly in danger of allowing our natural and cultural heritage to be destroyed in the march of so-called progress.[37]

It must therefore have been gratifying to him in his old age, after so many refusals and disappointments, to have finally been able to give real form to his ideas, to build as he had designed, in a pioneering manner, breaking new ground and discovering new possibilities. He made the best of his late opportunities and it is sad that he did not see any of his last great works complete.

In our chronological survey we had reached '64, as this was the year of the State Library competition. Largely as a result of the success of the Philharmonie Scharoun found himself again the recipient of various academic honours. In '64 he received the major prize of the Federation of German Architects, and in '65 the Auguste Perret prize and an honorary doctorate at Rome university. Despite this academic recognition literary coverage of his work remained sparse. He did not himself write generally about his work and he tended to discourage others from doing so. Being by nature a modest man he thought his work would speak for itself, which it has in Germany though not outside. Most of his projects were well documented one by one in German magazines, particularly in the Berlin based *Bauwelt*, and the Philharmonie was published in magazines throughout the world, but the only general

coverage of his work and philosophy was Margit Staber's short article in *Zodiac* of '62, which had a nearly incomprehensible English translation. Thus his international reputation was, and has remained, patchy; one finds him highly respected here yet totally unknown there. Very few people outside Germany seem to know much about his work.

Two new projects are listed for '65, the prize winning Wolfsburg theatre (p. 31) and the Rauher Kapf housing development in Böblingen (p. 53), both of which have now been realised. The remaining six projects listed in the Berlin Arts Academy catalogue of '67 belong to the year '66. They are the Zabel Krügerdamm block of flats (p. 51), a private house for a Doctor Torman in Bad Homburg, the AOK building on Mehringplatz (p. 105), the Architectural Faculty at Berlin Technical University (p. 87) and two church designs, the one for Wolfsburg covered earlier (p. 86) and another for a 'church of the transfiguration of Christ' at Berlin Schöneberg. It seems unlikely now that either church project will be realised.

The Berlin Church is remarkable among Scharoun's projects through having in its basic conception an attempt at conscious symbolism. It is true that he often

chose to describe his projects in terms of natural metaphors, The Valley and the Hill of the Berlin plan, for example, and the Vineyard Terraces of the Philharmonie, but seldom did he begin a project with the intention of representing something. Even in the case of the Romeo and Juliet flats the symbolism did not give rise to the conception, but rather followed it. However, in his Church of the Transfiguration, Scharoun set out to represent a 'tree of life' in his structure, and designed the roof to fan out from one single centrally placed column, with concrete 'branches' supporting the roof segments at different levels. This would have produced some very dramatic effects, with the daylight pouring in between the roof segments at a variety of different angles. A church is surely one of the building types in which conscious symbolism is most justifiable,

and it allowed Scharoun in this case to add richness without irrelevance.

The church site was an open space at a junction in a busy part of Berlin. Scharoun pushed the building up against the edge of the site to leave as much ground free as possible for a garden. He separated the bell-tower from the main structure and set it in the garden where it could be seen from, and ring down, the surrounding streets, and he also proposed that the tube station entrance should be incorporated in the base of this bell-tower. He made the church building sufficiently high and prominent to compete for attention with its neighbours, and because of its busy site he made it more aggressively angular and forthright than the gentle, peaceful Wolfsburg church designed in the same year (p. 86).

Opposite and left
Project for a 'Church of the Transfiguration of Christ', Berlin, 1966, ground floor plan and model.

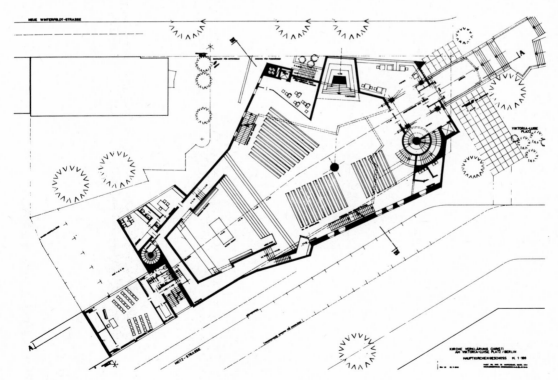

The year '66 is the last listed in the Berlin Arts Academy catalogue, so the few projects done between then and '72 have yet to be put in order. In the last years of his life Scharoun's output was limited by his own failing physical condition, and much of his energy was in any case taken up with the two large projects under construction, the state library and Wolfsburg theatre. The only major new projects to emerge were designs for a chamber music hall, a museum of musical instruments and an institute for musical research to be added to the Philharmonie, the high rise block Orplid at Böblingen, and the German Maritime Museum at Bremerhaven.

The Maritime Museum was commissioned and designed in '69 with the collaboration of Helmut Bohnsack, a local architect. It is now complete and was opened in Sept. '75. It seems strangely

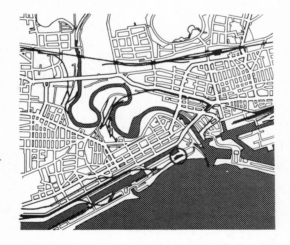

appropriate that this of all buildings, concerned as it is so essentially with his childhood home, should have been Scharoun's last major work. He felt deeply involved in the task and honoured to have been given the commission, and he expressed his feelings about the project in the following words:

The vital variety of this project, which is expressed in the structure and form of the building, reflects the character of its natural and cultural surroundings. It is the soul of the port and the heritage of the townspeople, reflecting the history of one of man's greatest challenges. The activity is indigenous to the place, situated as it is on the frontier between land and sea. Things determined by the environment in this way and things developed and evolved, depend on experience, practice and intuition as much as on scientific knowledge. The force of intuition has been with me since my youth in all my creative work, so it is a great pleasure for me to be allowed to plan this museum at Bremerhaven, the very place of origin of that creative motivation which has sustained me throughout my life.[38]

The museum is sited on a patch of land bounded on the east by the old harbour and on the west by a sea wall controlling the wide estuary of the river Weser. This places the building near the middle of the harbour complex, and close to the various old ships lying permanently at anchor in the old harbour which form a part of the exhibition.

The planning of the museum seems deceptively casual and proves difficult to analyse. This is because it grows out of a complex mixture of influences which is hard to unravel. In the examination of Scharoun's schools, theatres and concert halls at the beginning of this book we found definite hierarchies of organisation in the plans which make the planning process evident. In the case of the Philharmonie, for example, the plan grew outward from the centre. First the auditorium was designed according to internal considerations, then the foyer had to answer to the auditorium, and so on. In the case of the Maritime Museum there is no such obvious hierarchy in the programme, and none appears in the form of the building. Instead the parts come together almost simultaneously in an arrangement determined by a large number of factors at once. So, rather than starting from a basic overall concept in our analysis of the plan, we should start by considering the parts separately.

Some of the ships and parts of ships housed in the museum are relatively large, and required specially designed exhibition areas. Principal amongst these specialist areas is the Cog-house, the large rectangular portion of the building at its northern corner. This will contain the precious Bremen Cog, a medieval wooden ship some 24 metres in length which was discovered

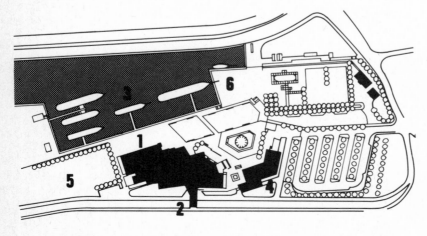

accidentally at the bottom of Bremen harbour during dredging operations in '62. It was remarkably well preserved by the mud that had encased it, and constituted a rare and exciting find, being the most complete example of its kind yet to emerge. The authorities rapidly arranged for it to be labelled and dismantled, intending to reconstruct it elsewhere, and it was stored away piece by piece in tanks of water. Reconstruction will be a long and arduous task, since the ancient waterlogged timber needs special preservative treatment if it is to dry out safely. First the ship must be put together again in an artificially fog-laden atmosphere, a task that is estimated to take four years, and then the whole thing must be immersed in preservative solution for twenty years so that it can become totally impregnated, after which it can finally be dried out. Owing to the ship's size and fragility it would be difficult to reconstruct it in a suitable workshop then afterwards move it to a permanent exhibition space, so it really requires a specialist building which can be first a fog-laden workshop, then a preservative bath, and finally part of a museum. Scharoun's Cog-house was designed to perform this function and the Cog is already being reconstructed there. It is sited at the northern end of the building, where it can be operated independently of the rest, having its own service road and entrance, its own technical facilities at basement level, and its own wing of offices. Until the reconstruction work is complete the Cog-house will be cut off from the rest of the building at ground, first and second floor levels by a wall which is indicated on the first floor plan as a dotted line.

The Cog-house is the most clearly defined element in the complex, a simple rectangular hall with a gallery on three sides and open on the fourth to allow the Cog to be seen as a whole. It has its own structure and is clearly articulated in the external form of the building. But despite this strong formal definition the ground floor space is continuous with the rest of the exhibition and plays an important part in the general spatial progression. Thus it upholds one of the basic rules of organic architecture – that part should have an identity of its own and yet belong to the whole.

Other parts of the complex can be seen as definite entities but are not as independent as the Cog-house. The office and library block, the porter's flat, the partitionable lecture hall, the line of workshops: all of these have conventional plan forms which hardly need be explained. What is curious is the way in which they fit together. As I stated earlier, this is not just a simple matter of slotting in the parts one by one, but a matter of juggling with them all until an arrangement

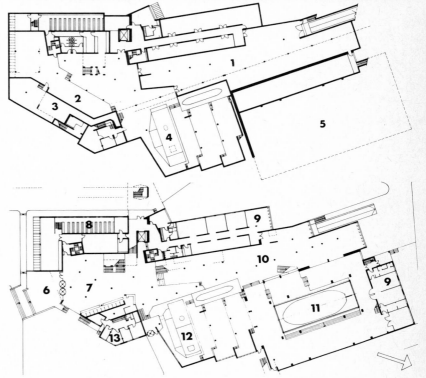

is found where all aspects of their interrelationships are satisfactory. Here is a short list of some of the determining factors:

(a) There are two public entrances, one on the ground floor at the southern end relating to the visitor's car park and the best footpath to town, the other at first floor level linking up with the promenade along

Below
First floor plan:
14, administration; 15, special exhibition; 16, exhibition; 17, lecture hall; 18, roof; 19, cog-house.

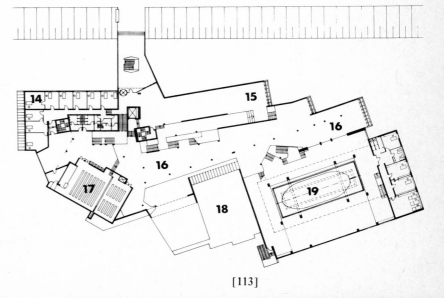

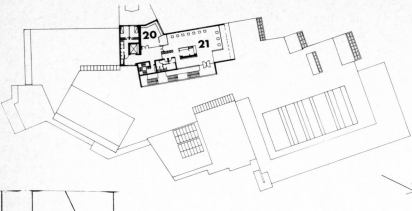

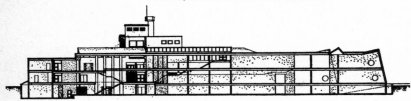

Second and third floor plans:
20, radar room 'ship's bridge';
21, refreshment room.

Section.

the sea wall. The axis of the ground floor entrance runs through the building and the main staircase system relates to it. The corner enclosed between the two entrances forms the library and administration block.

(b) To be easily accessible to visitors, lecture hall, library, and administrative offices are placed near the entrances. The porter's desk controls the main entrance, and his flat is close behind.

(c) The exhibition areas on either side of the Coghouse face north-east and north-west, and are provided with vast slanting northlight windows.

(d) The administrative offices and refreshment room take advantage of the westward view over the sea wall. The library placed beneath, where the view is obstructed by the sea wall, does not need a view. The radar room, which must overlook the shipping channel, is placed high on the western side.

(e) The ground floor exhibition spaces are arranged in a downward clockwise spiral to end up at basement level without a harsh break in level.

(f) The massing of the building is arranged to focus on the upper entrance, as seen from the sea wall.

These factors help to explain the placing of the various elements, but they do not explain the shapes or angle changes. In fact the whole plan is based on one single axial shift which develops between the axis of the main entrance and the line of the sea wall. The axis of the main entrance is itself set as a careful compromise between facing the car park, and following the line of the most direct footpath into town.

At a more detailed level the angle changes seem prompted by the usual considerations concerning smoothness of circulation flow. I will pick out one example, the staircase in the L-shaped administration and library block which is twisted around in relation to the rectangular layout of surrounding parts. On the ground floor this twist produces two tapering passages: one divides at the narrow end to feed a staircase and the other has the congestion of two doors at its wide end and only a single one at the narrow end, so both are tapered to advantage. On the first floor congestion at the corner of the L-shaped passage, where there are several doors, has again been avoided. Also the change in wall angle outside the staircase is sympathetic to the swing round of circulation outside the lecture hall.

But these are humble things: let us leave them on

German Maritime Museum, Bremerhaven, 1969–75. South side of the museum from the sea wall promenade.

one side to progress to deeper issues, and come closer to the heart of the matter, for I have scarcely mentioned the building's real virtues. Above and beyond all the considerations so far voiced are some rather less definable issues which are not less important. How can one convey in words the wonderful quality of the exhibition spaces, where shifts in level, changes of daylight, and the flow of volume into volume combine in a breathtaking progression?

In Scharoun's earlier work we could just about trace his thinking and understand how these things came about, but here he has left us far behind. His awareness and judgement have reached a stage where he can juggle with an impossible range of solutions and pick the right one, and where he knows just how much to push a wall this way or that, or how much to angle it around to get exactly the required effect, when we would know no difference. Other architects have done it, but never before with such a wide vocabulary. We must look too at the outside of the museum. It has a rhythmic quality that seems highly appropriate to its purpose and which is not evident in other Scharoun buildings. How he gauged what it should be and how

he controlled what it became, are quite beyond analysis. Again, when we look at the building from the seaward side it has a distinctly ship-like character and massing, which was obviously intended, and this again is gauged to perfection – the effect is neither too obvious nor too weak.

It is these things above all else that make this building so remarkable. It displays that tranquillity and rare

Top
Museum behind sea wall as seen from beach.

Main entrance at night.
Left
Main flight of stairs which acts as a spine of the building.

Below
View from radar tower.

perfection of judgement that one finds only among the late works of the greatest artists, when the passions and vigour of youth have vanished, and the time of earnest demonstration is over, when all the accumulated wisdom of a lifetime blossoms forth for the last time in one perfect flower. There is a kind of spiritual optimism in such works for which we must ever be grateful. They are the quiet fountains of hope to which we can always return when weary of the world, fountains which refresh our humanity so that, when we must rejoin the fray we do so with replenished energy and a rediscovered sense of purpose.

Scharoun was always totally committed to his work and to what he felt it meant in social and political terms. It remained to the end his inspiration and his delight. He never retired, and when he had finally become too weak to make his way to his office, he had the drawings brought to his home. Fate had been kind to Scharoun in his old age: she allowed him to build

more than ever before and she did not finally break off his work rudely at an inopportune moment, but rather rounded it off in a cyclic fashion, bringing him back with his final masterpiece to the haunts of his youth. She was also kind in the way she let him grow old for, though he suffered the usual physical disabilities, he retained his clarity of mind and judgement to the last. She let him live just long enough to give definite shape to his final work, but she had set a price on her kindness and the price was that he should never see his last works complete. He died on 25 November 1972 at the age of seventy-nine.

At first it must seem very sad that the triumphs of a life's work were held for ever from the view of their creator, but we find them so well considered and so precisely conceived that he must have known every inch and must have seen them in that even more gloriously finished state that only the imagination knows. Perhaps in those last moments of existence he walked

The deck of the *Crown-Prince*,
left, is at ground floor level, but a
staircase within the ship leads
down to cabins and an exit in the
basement.

[116]

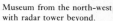

Museum from the north-west with radar tower beyond.

of earnest human activity and bathed in that carefully captured and preserved *himmellicht*; the astonishing theatre at Wolfsburg growing out of its green hillside like a great rock, softened only by those long delicate wings stretching out across the grass as if to grasp at nature. Finally, perhaps, the eye of the imagination would turn fondly to that port imbued forever with the brightness and mystery of childhood, where it would find among the busy quays with their smells of salt and tar and cries of gulls, a quiet resting place for the ships of old and a monument to those who had sailed in them: a gentle building in shades of grey softly lit by the northern sky: inside, the levels, spaces, shafts of light, responsive to a master's hand.

He surveys it for the last time with the satisfaction of knowing it a task well done, needing no further refinement. Levels slide into each other gracefully, light falls here with freshness and there with surprise; space is free, yet happily obedient. Satisfied that all this is in order, he lingers on a while to drift outside where a sea breeze blows briskly and plays his eternal games with his friend the sea, whisking him into a flurry of excitement then racing him to the shore. The sky is wild and grey and agitated. Here and there the sun peeps through for a moment and sends strong rays gliding across the land, making fields suddenly greener, then leaving them to fade like the end of a dream. The sun's rays skim on across the sea, making him sparkle with delight. All is as fresh, bright and wild as it was all those years ago when childish voices strove against the roar of the wind.

Multiple level changes on the east side of the building where ground floor spirals down into basement.

East side of the building; main entrance left, cog-house right.

again around those great projects whose bare shells were just beginning to show signs of life, and saw them finished: the great majestic reading room of the library, with its profusion of levels and staircases, full

Chapter 11: An Evaluation

Now that we are familiar with the architecture of Hans Scharoun and the generative processes behind it, certain questions naturally arise. How well do the buildings work? What can we learn from Scharoun? Should we try to follow his approach? How does it compare with other approaches? In this final chapter I shall attempt to answer these questions and further to clarify the historical perspective in which I have chosen to see Scharoun's work.

Whether we love or hate his architecture, we must at least admit that Scharoun held a very identifiable and comparatively extreme theoretical position. Such a position provides the critic with a convenient reference point as he can develop from it various comparative arguments and polemics. Polemic is one of the critic's most useful tools. By pointing out the contrast between two extremes he can clarify issues which may be difficult to recognise in a milder form, and whichever side he supports he tends to do both a service by making their views known and getting them better understood – as long as he gets the arguments right. In my chapter on the philosophy of 'new building' I drew a polemic between Häring's position and that of Le Corbusier on the issue of responsive versus imposed aesthetics, and I picked up the same argument a couple of times during my analyses of Scharoun's projects. Now I shall return to the conflicts between 'new building' and the International Style and draw some alternative polemics based on different though interrelated issues. The first has as its opposite poles Mies

van der Rohe, and 'new building' as represented by both Häring and Scharoun. The issue at stake can be described as flexibility versus identity.

In the early twenties Häring shared an office with Mies. Their relationship was by all accounts quite friendly but they were in constant disagreement over matters of architectural theory. Mies always held that buildings change function frequently and should be of a generalised type which can be adapted as necessary. Häring, in contrast, searched tirelessly for the 'essential form' by trying to define each function as accurately as possible and to design specifically for that function. In his house plans he pursued this philosophy to its ultimate conclusion and ended up almost prescribing a way of life: here you will sit when you write letters to auntie; there you will do your sewing. Mies rightly criticised this policy for being far too specific and thereby placing unnecessary constraints on the occupants. 'Make your rooms large, Hugo,' he said, 'then you can use them however you like.'[39] In his own work Mies took his philosophy of flexibility to ever greater and greater extremes. He eventually produced as a house a neutral glass box which supposedly would allow total freedom. This turned out to be a jack of all trades and master of none, and Mies became involved in a lawsuit with his client, who considered the house uninhabitable. He had undoubtedly gone far too far: there is some advantage in making buildings flexible in terms of use but, unless you also make them movable, the north sides always face north and the south sides south, providing quite different lighting conditions which must be taken into account if such rudimentary problems as excessive solar heat gain are to be avoided. Apart from such humble considerations one can also make out a good case that varying degrees of privacy and enclosure are psychologically necessary in domestic buildings, and will continue to be so.

Scharoun came close to Häring in his attitude to domestic planning but he never went quite to the extreme. He would design into a house plan numerous built-in cupboards, and he would also accommodate large items of furniture such as pianos, sofas and dining tables, but the disposition of smaller items was left quite flexible. In his room layouts he often provided sliding screens to give some flexibility of use. Indeed, this kind of limited flexibility with well defined options is a common feature of his work. I visited two Scharoun houses, both built in the thirties: the Baensch house in Berlin described in my opening chapter, and the Hoffmeyer house in Bremerhaven. Mrs Baensch still occupies the first floor of the house

Hans Scharoun (front right), Margit Scharoun (front left) and Ludwig Mies van der Rohe (front centre) together in Berlin at the topping-out ceremony of the National Gallery, 1967. Photo credit: Reinhard Friedrich.

Baensch house, 1935, south side.

built for her late husband, and the Hoffmeyers still occupy the other house. The ground floor of the Baensch house is occupied by a doctor and his family. He said of it: 'When I first set eyes on this room I knew that this was the house for me'. I asked the occupants of both houses how they felt about the built-in furniture and specifically designed rooms, and whether they would prefer a more flexible arrangement. In both cases they seemed surprised by the question and expressed considerable satisfaction with the existing situation. Neither house had been subjected to any major alterations. This is by no means statistical evidence, but it proves at least that some people prefer very specifically designed houses.

'Make your rooms large,' said Mies. Of course, in the past flexibility was often achieved through sheer size. If domestic rooms are made 25 feet square the proportion of space occupied by furniture tends to remain relatively small, leaving most of the floor area vacant. So circulation can take place more or less at random, needing no specifically designed space. Under such generous conditions room shape and proportion are not accurately determined by functional considerations and geometrical aesthetics come to the fore. Nowadays with high building costs and many more people to accommodate the floor area available per person has shrunk considerably and we have to use it more efficiently. The bedroom becomes so small that we have to juggle with the dimensions to fit in the bed. Not only does this mean that sizes and proportions have to be determined functionally rather than aesthetically, it also means we have to start designing circulation space rather than just expecting leftover space to work. This pushes us towards a policy of specific design whether we like it or not.

Scharoun was a great master in the design of tight economical flats, and there is little doubt that by designing very specifically he made the best use of the space available. On the whole his housing schemes have been very successful in spite of their unorthodox rooms. The success story of Romeo and Juliet is quite entertaining. Romeo and Juliet, Salute and Orplid were all private developments in which the flats were sold separately to owner-occupiers. When Romeo was completed and occupied in '57 six flats were offered to Stuttgart furniture dealers, who were invited to furnish these unusual rooms as best they could, as show-flats. When they were opened to the public, interest grew until people were queuing down through the building and out along the road. With all this interest sales of flats in Juliet, then still under construction, increased markedly. Juliet was completed and

Hoffmeyer house, 1935, view from garden.

occupied in '59. The commercial success of the venture prompted the building of Salute and Orplid, which have proved equally popular.

The strongest criticism of a Scharoun building by its inhabitants over lack of flexibility that I have heard concerned the school at Marl. The essential problem is quite simple. The school was designed shortly before the German educational system underwent a considerable change in organisation, so class groupings and pupils' ages have changed and the building is not used as intended. Apart from these organisational changes classes are about 30 per cent larger than originally envisaged, and teachers complained that the classrooms were too small. Only building oversize would have prevented this problem though, and that would have been very largely an economic matter.

In general the teachers I spoke to at the Marl school agreed that the building was a pleasant and inspiring place to work in, but some felt that the money had been

spent in the wrong places, and were particularly indig-
nant about that spent on the assembly hall, for it is
not often used and as yet it has not become the kind
of cultural centre for the locality that it was intended
to be. Part of the reason for this is that access to it cannot be cut off physically from the rest of the school,
and thus its use by outsiders presents security problems. Another criticism by a teacher concerned the
outdoor spaces. The fragmentary form of the building
produces numerous separate garden areas which have
been generously landscaped. For the children it is a
paradise but for staff trying to control them in break
periods it is difficult. One teacher frankly admitted that
he would prefer a single, bleak, open playground
where he could see what every child was up to. He
summed up his criticisms of the school rather percep-
tively by suggesting that the whole conception was too
idealistic: 'It is a wonderful school for ideal children,
but these children are far from ideal'.

Of course Scharoun intended his schools to express
social ideals: that much is obvious from his own writings about them, and it is surely important to encourage idealism in educational buildings. He was certainly
not the first architect to suggest that the experience
of buildings has an educational effect on those who use
them. Pugin had suggested it a hundred years earlier
in his *True Principles*. After contrasting 'English catholic colleges' with 'modern collegiate buildings' (see
p. 89) with illustrations, he continued as follows:

How is it possible to expect that the race of men who proceed
from these factories of learning (modern collegiate buildings)
will possess the same feelings as those who anciently went
forth from the catholic structures of Oxford and Win-
chester.[40]

Much of Scharoun's architectural philosophy, and indeed everything that Pugin argued in the name of propriety, depends on a belief in this kind of causal link
between buildings and human experience. It is the
functional justification for providing buildings with
specific identities related to their purposes, and it conflicts with Mies's concept of open ended flexibility
because, without a specific purpose, a building cannot
have an identity related to its purpose. You can trade
identity for flexibility or vice versa but you cannot have
both at once. Some of the shortcomings of the Marl
school could have been avoided in a more flexible design, but most of the strong sense of place and spatial
hierarchy in Scharoun's building would not have come
about. Perhaps the advantages outweigh the disadvantages: it will always be a matter of opinion.

Scharoun's other school, the Geschwister Scholl
girls' school at Lünen, has had a happier history. Its
smaller size may be a major determining factor in its
greater success, as it certainly seems much more intimate in scale than the school at Marl, and the idea of
the *Klassenwohnung* seems more tempting. The principal of the school is obviously a Scharoun fan and has
nothing but praise for it and the way it works. The
one other teacher that I spoke to there had only one
real criticism, that the staff library was far too small
and that Scharoun had been more concerned with the
accommodation of the pupils than of the staff. There
may be some truth in this as the staff quarters are tacked
on to the end of the plan in a way that suggests they
were considered last.

Although Scharoun stood very much against Mies's
concept of total flexibility he nevertheless made his
buildings flexible in some limited ways. In both the
schools, he planned the classrooms to allow the
greatest possible variation in seating layout, and this
facility is well used in practice. In a book on the
behavioural basis of design entitled *Personal Space*,
Robert Sommer, an American psychologist, has
stressed the great importance of this kind of flexibility,
having conducted comparative tests on the effects of
classroom layout on pupils' performances.[41] He also
stressed the importance of good lighting conditions in
classrooms, another factor which Scharoun was greatly
concerned with. The sort of psychological evidence
presented by Sommer does demonstrate scientifically,
for those who must have a scientific demonstration,
that the kind of concerns Scharoun based his classroom designs on do have a very real value.

I have not yet done with concepts of flexibility and
the arguments between Mies and 'new building'. As I
have mentioned earlier in this book Mies's National

Mies van der Rohe, National
Gallery, Berlin, 1968. View from
north west.

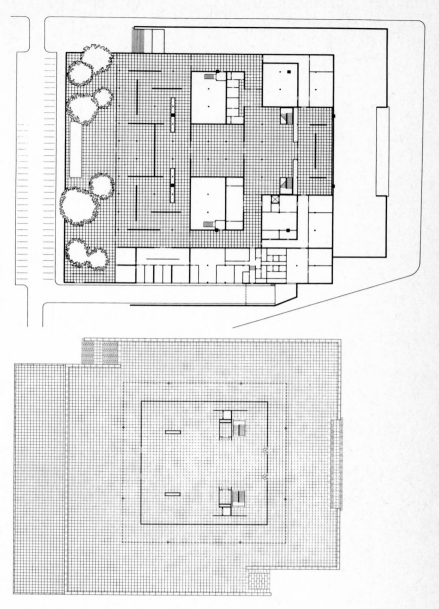

Gallery in Berlin stands close to the Philharmonie, and the contrast between these two buildings can provide further fuel for our discussion. The Philharmonie could scarcely be more specific to its purpose or less flexible. It could just about be used as a meeting hall or theatre but further it could not be pushed. But does this matter? How often do concert halls change function completely? Mies's National Gallery goes to the opposite extreme. It is supposed to be a universal building and because of its intended flexibility it has many functional shortcomings. Will this flexibility ever be used? At root is functional flexibility the primary issue over which these buildings differ or are there some more fundamental considerations involved?

I need scarcely repeat what the Philharmonie is about and how it was designed, all that was covered in some detail in Chapter 4. But how well does it work? In general I think I can fairly say that it is a great success. The unorthodox layout has been welcomed by many prominent musicians. Pierre Boulez, for example, has long felt the limitations of conventional halls, which, he claimed,

were built for another purpose, and therefore you use them with great difficulty. The frame is not right, the disposition of the audience is not right, everything is wrong. It is better not to fight against these conditions, but to use another place ... The Berlin Philharmonie is the only hall I know which is conceived in different terms.[42]

The acoustics of the Philharmonie are generally considered good, though the balance of instruments is poor in some places, an inevitable result of the 'in the round' layout. Perhaps most importantly the psychological effects that Scharoun was aiming for, the sense of unified musical experience in the hall and the dramatic contrast between hall and foyer, have come off to perfection and seem widely appreciated if not always understood. The public is most critical of the exterior of the building, which is considered by many people to be ugly. It has been nicknamed, not I think without affection, *Zirkus Karajani* ('Karajan's circus') which is a play on the name of a popular German

circus, *Zirkus Sarasani*. What nobody can deny is that it has a great deal of character and is unlikely to be confused with other buildings – it makes a good landmark. Various criticisms have been levelled at the Philharmonie concerning its complexity and the difficulties encountered in constructing it. That it was difficult to build cannot be denied, but it was built on time and remarkably cheaply: at 17 million DM in '63 it was the cheapest concert hall of its size in Europe at around that time.

Mies's National Gallery is somewhat smaller in over-all floor area than the Philharmonie but, because of the construction and materials chosen, it cost considerably more (25 million DM in '68), which only goes to show that simplicity is not necessarily cheap,

Mies van der Rohe, National Gallery, Berlin, 1968, basement.

Ground floor plan. Credit: Gerd Hatje Verlag.

Perspective drawing of basic structure. Credit: Gerd Hatje Verlag.

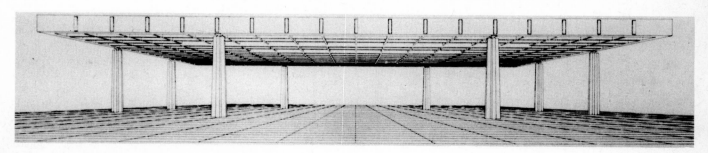

that complexity is not necessarily expensive, and that 'less' generally costs more. The gallery was one of Mies's last works. In the early sixties the German authorities realised with some embarrassment that they had no postwar building by one of their greatest architects, and that he was unlikely to live much longer. They therefore gave him the gallery commission with few strings attached and a generous budget. We can take it that Mies built according to his best principles and without compromise, so the gallery can fairly be seen as representative of his theories.

Mies chose to bury the main part of his building, the whole of the permanent collection, underground, and to build on the surface a simple steel and glass structure to a design which he had previously proposed as an office building for Bacardi in Cuba. The resulting complex makes a plausible art gallery, but certainly not a good one. Both of the two main design criteria normally associated with art galleries, lighting and circulation, were ignored in the basic conception and, consequently, the paintings are not shown off to advantage and the exhibition cannot be seen as a progression. From a functionalist point of view this is unforgivable, but let us apply broader criteria of judgement. If functional efficiency has been lost, what has been gained – flexibility?

Wolfgang Pehnt, a critic of decidedly neo-classical sympathies, wrote of the gallery that it was 'better suited to some purpose as yet unspecified'. One might add 'as yet uninvented' for it is hard to imagine what the building could be ideal for. But in any case how likely is an art gallery to change function? Surely a National Gallery with a permanent collection must be among the most enduring of institutions. However there is one way in which such galleries do require to be flexible: they tend to expand in size as the collection grows. Ironically, Mies has not allowed for this. Cer-

tainly it would not be physically difficult to expand the gallery, but it would be aesthetically difficult because the building is so symmetrical and finite. On this issue the tables are turned. The Philharmonie is surely one of the most inflexible of buildings regarding a complete change of function, but it is easily expandable because it was designed in an essentially cumulative manner. When the planned chamber music hall and museum of musical instruments have been added to it as intended, the overall composition of the complex will have been changed, but not disrupted. The Philharmonie is more aesthetically flexible than Mies's gallery. Here, incidentally, is another parallel with the arguments between nineteenth century Gothicists and Classicists: Gothic was cumulative and could be added to; Classical was finite, a statement complete in itself.

Mies's gallery is not functionally efficient and it is not flexible in the one way which is likely to matter practically. What, then, is this curious building about? Is it an expression of pure structure or construction? The structure is decidedly crude and the roof suffers a deflexion of about four inches; it certainly has none of the purity and logic of a Nervi structure. And construction? Certain parts of it are displayed prominently, the column bearings for example, but other parts of the mechanism of the building, I am thinking particularly of the services, are deliberately hidden. The apparent simplicity has only been obtained by a lot of careful and expensive concealment. Some people have mistakenly seen those column bearings as an expression of steel construction. I say mistakenly because the earlier version of the same building, the office in Cuba, was supposed to be built in concrete and yet its form and structure are virtually identical. This is a strong reminder of that piece of classical theory that I quoted in an earlier chapter concerning the transformation of the Greek temple from timber to stone, the form itself being considered more important than the materials used. As Fiedler put it,

materials and constructions continue to recede, while the form, which belongs to the intellect, continues to develop towards an increasingly independent existence.[43]

This is surely what Mies was about, pure form, universal form, not for practical but for aesthetic reasons. In an age when practical justifications are respected above aesthetic ones the notion of universal flexibility was a helpful piece of propaganda, but it was not the real issue at stake. It was, rather, a red herring to keep the rationalists happy, and to justify an abidication from all architectural problems except those that he chose particularly to concern himself with.

Mies van der Rohe, Bacardi office building project, Cuba 1958. Eight columns and a coffered roof as with the Art Gallery. Credit: Lund Humphries Publishers Ltd.

Mies of all modern architects stands most firmly in the Classical tradition. His gallery can be seen as a kind of twentieth century descendant of the Greek temple and, arguably, an art gallery can legitimately be treated as a kind of temple, for the aesthetic and spiritual discipline implied in its form are not inappropriate to that function. But they would be inappropriate to most other functions, and that is where Mies's philosophy falls apart. The Berlin Gallery happens to serve an important aesthetic purpose, and its existence can be justified on the grounds that its aesthetic virtues outweigh its high cost and functional shortcomings, a view to which I readily subscribe despite the criticisms I have made. However, if we are asked to accept it as a 'universal' building rather than as an art gallery, we must object because of the implications. Imagine a whole series of these structures used for a variety of purposes: apart from the fact that they would be excessively expensive and functionally inefficient there would be no way of telling what purpose each served and of distinguishing between them. They would be meaningless.

Now if we go back to the arguments between Mies and Häring over flexibility it becomes evident that the issue was not fundamentally a practical one, for it must have been obvious to both of them that from a strictly practical point of view a compromise between the two extremes was inevitable. But as I have already pointed out, Mies's arguments about flexibility allowed him to abdicate from most functional considerations so that he could pursue the pure forms and aesthetic disciplines that he felt so committed to. He could design buildings without functions, so functional problems were to him merely an encumbrance, a nuisance. But for Häring on the other hand, who rejected aesthetics, functional considerations were the life-blood of the design process, they were vital, without them he could not operate. Where they were vague or nonexistent he had to invent them, or at least to interpret the situation very liberally. From a strictly practical point of view of course this seems senseless, but Häring was not such a keen functionalist merely for practical reasons. What he was really after was a specific identity or meaning for each of his buildings, not an imposed meaning but an inevitable inherent meaning. When he rejected aesthetic doctrine he did not do so because he thought it was rubbish, he had a considerable respect for it, as his writings about 'Architecture', and indeed his very acknowledgement of that title, indicate. He rejected it because he realised that it conflicted with the kind of identity which he sought, and he thought identity more important than beauty, expression of

purpose more important than expression of intellectual ideals.

If for a moment we take a neutral position in this argument and accept that identity and beauty are equally important aims, Häring still has the edge on Mies because his pursuit of identity does not conflict with practical functions, being inevitably allied to them, whereas Mies's aesthetic pursuits quite often do conflict with practical functions, as we have seen in the case of his Berlin Gallery. Mies never really faced the problems inherent in this conflict because of a basic contradiction in his thinking. He did not always admit his aesthetic interests and, while one half of his mind was pursuing pure form, the other half believed that he was producing buildings so neutral, so anonymous, so universal, that they would almost fade away into the background. The latter idea, though attractive, is quite fallacious, for the Berlin Gallery, to take a particular case, does not fade away into the background at all. On the contrary, it is an immensely strong and memorable formal statement. The only buildings which ever really do fade into the background are very ordinary traditional buildings which are unmemorable because they are unremarkable and just like everything else around them.

If the pursuit of beauty in architecture conflicted neither with functional requirements nor with the expression of purpose or, to put it another way, if 'aesthetics' was an entirely independent ingredient which could be added to the architectural stew to enrich it without spoiling what was already there, then we could argue for its universal adoption. But as it is, we often have to choose between beauty and functional efficiency or between beauty and identity, so we must always arrive at a compromise of some kind. In certain cases, such as that of the Berlin Gallery, the aesthetic statement is probably justified, but in other cases, such as housing, it probably is not.

When Mies was designing his Lakeside Drive apartment blocks he became concerned that the curtains put up by residents would be visible behind the windows of their flats and would disrupt the simple, perfect statement of his steel and glass façade. He therefore had blinds of a uniform type installed throughout and, to keep a semblance of geometrical order in the façade pattern, these were arranged to stop only in the up, down and halfway up positions. This is not only practically inconvenient, it also completely prevents the occupants of the flats from expressing themselves in any way on the exterior of the building. It is dictatorship through architecture and has been severely criticised as such. So aesthetic purity conflicts not only with practical functions and with a building's expression of its purpose, it also represses the expression of the occupants. For even if they are not actively prevented from making their mark they so obviously disrupt the aesthetic statement that the building is making that they are forced to be hostile to it.

So far this argument has revolved around Mies alone because I have been taking his work as the extreme test case. But many of the arguments can be applied equally to much of the work of Le Corbusier and Gropius. In '26 Le Corbusier built a small housing estate at Pessac, near Bordeaux, in the simple cubist style that he had invented in the early 1920s. The houses had the usual Corbusier features of the time, pilotis, roof-gardens, wide horizontal windows, etc. Over the years they have been extensively modified by their owners: pitched roofs have replaced flat; narrow windows have been put in; spaces between pilotis have been filled in and all kinds of decorative features have been added. The place has been changed almost beyond recognition. Now at one level it can be argued that the scheme was highly successful because it proved so convertible, but that was certainly not Corbusier's intention. No doubt he would be distressed to see what has happened, because the aesthetic statement he was trying to make has been completely destroyed: it has been eroded by the realities of everyday life; purity has given way to messy vitality. This only proves that the aesthetic was quite inappropriate in the first place. Corbusier insisted on treating everything at the same aesthetic level, the heroic level if you like, and in the end the only buildings he designed in which the aesthetic discipline is thoroughly in tune with the purpose served are those devoted to religion and the arts.

In the work of Gropius too the conflict between aesthetics and function is evident. When Kandinsky complained of poor lighting in his studio at the Bauhaus, for instance, Gropius refused to make any changes on the grounds that his façade would be spoiled if he did. It was also at Gropius's Bauhaus more than anywhere else that the idea of total design, everything within the pure consistency of one style, was pursued. Aesthetic quality was the essential aim, on the basis that beautiful objects would have a universal appeal and that everyone would therefore want them. The vital error in this kind of thinking was the failure to realise that people like to be different. Giving them all identical objects or lining them up in identical dwellings, however beautiful those objects or dwellings are, is like forcing them to wear a uniform – it is repressive. Untidy, unruly humanity inevitably breaks out of such

closed systems wherever it is able to, as indeed has happened at Pessac.

In the words 'closed systems' lies the root of the problem. The aesthetic that Mies, Le Corbusier and Gropius pursued in the twenties was too finite, too pure, too inflexible. Its purity was such that any alien intrusion could only be seen as discordant. Their buildings could not admit growth and change, even the effects of wind and rain detracted from their heroic character rather than adding to it. When the freshness had worn off they just looked shabby, whereas an organic building such as Häring's cowshed just mellows with age and seems to sink more comfortably into the landscape as the years go by. Häring understood only too well what the heroic aesthetic was about and what its limitations were:

Geometry brings forth the idea of Architecture. It celebrates timeless immutable space. It rejects any element of movement as contrary to the finite and absolute which is its domain.

In a world which is constantly changing, man needs to set up absolute reference points to which he can cling and upon which he can rely. This is one of his basic religious needs, and it is in consequence a basic aesthetic need. Man needs also to set up physical representation of the unchanging abstract laws of the intellect, for until he imposes them upon the world they exist only in his mind. Besides, finite perfect arrangements also appeal to man because his intellect can grasp them totally, whereas organic things only reveal to him deeper and deeper mysteries. For these reasons the finite aesthetic is a recurrent feature in human culture, but in the past it has generally been applied in a strict form only to buildings of great religious or political significance: it has never been applied in a strict form universally. A similar line of argument can be found in the writings of Wilhelm Worringer, one of Häring's intellectual forebears (see p. 88). According to Worringer's central thesis aesthetic motivation oscillates between the 'urge to empathy' and the 'urge to abstraction'.

Whereas the precondition for the urge to empathy is a happy pantheistic relationship of confidence between man and the phenomena of the external world, the urge to abstraction is the outcome of a great inner unrest inspired in man by the phenomena of the outside world; in a religious respect it corresponds to a strongly transcendental tinge to all notions. We might describe this state as an immense spiritual dread of space ...

Tormented by the entangled inter-relationship and flux of the phenomena of the outer world, certain peoples were dominated by an immense need for tranquillity. The happiness they sought from art did not consist in the possibility of projecting themselves into the things of the outer world, of enjoying themselves in them, but in the possibility of taking the individual thing of the external world out of its arbitrariness and seeming fortuitousness, of eternalising it by approximation to abstract forms and, in this manner, of finding a point of tranquillity and a refuge from appearances. Their most powerful urge was, so to speak, to wrest the object of the external world out of its natural context, out of the unending flux of being, to purify it of all its dependence upon life, i.e. of everything about it that was arbitrary, to render it necessary and irrefragable, to approximate it to its *absolute* value.[45]

In this century the rate of change of Western culture has increased enormously, so the undue emphasis placed on the finite and absolute by most modern architects may be a reaction against what the futurists called a world of 'steel, fever, pride and headlong speed'. Certainly Mies admitted that one of his fundamental aims was 'to create order out of the desperate confusion of our time'.[46] It is above all the quality of calm and timelessnesss that makes Mies's buildings impressive. His insistence on flexibility might seem at first sight to conflict with the pursit of the finite and absolute, but in fact it supports it. Only by making his buildings capable of serving an impossibly wide range of functions could he be sure that they would not be pulled down or converted. He evidently intended they should stand unchanged for ever.

Unlike Mies, Scharoun and Häring were prepared to accept 'the desperate confusion of our time' in all its complexity and to find their particular order in each task as it arose. They saw buildings as continuous with the life that they contained and as integral with the landscape and townscape in which they stood. Their buildings were not neat, precise and detached like International Style buildings, but dissolved into their surroundings and apparently senseless if seen out of context. In consequence such buildings do not come out well in photographs for photographs do lift buildings out of context, whereas buildings designed out of context often come over better in photographs than in reality.

The approach of Scharoun and Häring to architecture, and indeed their whole state of mind, was open-ended and accommodating. They felt drawn to the infinite rather than to the finite. Scharoun was writing, right at the beginning of his career that

Knowledge that leads us on a narrow path does not satisfy us. If it does in any way lead us to infinity, it is to a measurable segment, to a finite infinity, to disappointment due to isolation.[47]

Meanwhile Häring felt that a major cultural shift was taking place away from the finite and absolute towards the open-ended. He thought that the use of modern materials in tension, implying movement, was symptomatic of this shift and significantly he saw the discovery of relativity as a part of the general trend:

The idea of the abstract, the immovable, the static is being replaced by that of life, of movement: being gives way to becoming. This change is universal, all-embracing. Take one example: in mathematics, Albert Einstein had attacked the principle of the absolute and ousted it from the realm of exact science also.[48]

Scharoun and Häring's open-ended approach has some considerable advantages. Above all, it accommodates growth and change and provides an environment whose principal qualities are richness and relevance rather than great aesthetic consistency. The rarified purity which cannot accommodate life is thus avoided, and untidy imperfect humanity is more at home. In Scharoun's flats the different coloured curtains in the windows do not conflict with the quality of the architecture, rather they add to it. He tended to welcome the expression of the inhabitants in his buildings. In his school at Lünen, for example, he recommended that the girls be allowed to paint murals on the corridor

A corridor in the Geschwister Scholl School, Lünen, 1958–62. The girls are encouraged to decorate their school with murals, as seen here on the left.

walls, and this they have done. And unlike the Bauhaus architects Scharoun did not believe in total one-man design. In the Philharmonie the interior decoration, the foyer floor pattern, the stained glass windows, the sculpture on the roof, and the landscaping were all delegated to other designers and artists. When I asked his wife whether he designed any furniture, she replied simply, 'It was not necessary'.

Scharoun's principal interest in architecture was the organisation of space; the construction of a building was always secondary. Consequently the constructional detailing in his buildings is very variable in quality: it all seems to work adequately, but some details are inelegant. In his detailing Scharoun seems to have followed the path of expediency, and this certainly has some advantages. One of the main reasons why his buildings were not on the whole exceptionally expensive, despite their irregularity and complexity, was that he did not insist on fussy difficult details and was prepared in some cases to change the design to cheapen construction. Thus the Philharmonie was originally intended to have a concrete shell roof, but it was built with a double skin truss roof to save money. He would not allow changes, however, if he believed they would threaten the basic conception. For instance he fought the authorities to the point of threatening resignation when they suggested that the Berlin State Library should have ordinary rooflights rather than northlights.

Over the exposure of services Scharoun could be more brutal than the Brutalists, not by self-consciously trying to display pipes or ducts but just by putting them where necessary without caring about untidiness. When the ventilating engineers working on the Berlin library tried to work out where to put their ducts across the northlight roof of the canteen they could find nowhere to conceal them, so they came back to Scharoun after a great deal of deliberation and told him that the ducts would have to run along the inside of the roof, there being nowhere else to put them. 'Well, why not?' replied Scharoun.

Scharoun's rather loose attitude toward construction has been much criticised by architects, indeed he has been accused of being out of touch with his time because he made construction subservient to architectural space rather than vice versa. But surely this is the right way round: we should decide what we want to build before we decide how to build it. Technology has always limited architectural possibilities and probably always will, but it should not of itself dictate architectural solutions. In this century we have a wider range of constructional possibilities than ever before: but instead of becoming an ever more versatile servant of architecture technology has all too often become a tyrannical master. The building turns into a machine with its own raison d'être. Scharoun's buildings seem senseless to those who understand buildings only as machines because they can see no reason for the complexity and irregularity of the forms used. If they cannot see the spatial concepts to which the construction is subservient then the construction itself must seem pointless. But once one realises what Scharoun is trying to do it makes a great deal of sense, and one can fairly argue that far from being out of touch with his time Scharoun is one of the few architects who have really taken advantage of the potential flexibility of reinforced concrete construction, and that through so doing he has created spaces of a fluidity unprecedented in architectural history.

There remains one further aspect of the conflict between the International Style and 'new building' that I must introduce here. This time the polemic runs between Scharoun and Häring on the one hand and Hannes Meyer on the other, and the argument concerns the state of mind known as Rationalism. Meyer succeeded Gropius as head of the Bauhaus in '28, the year in which he also published the manifesto from which the extracts quoted below are taken. I have chosen Meyer as the arch-rationalist because he expresses that state of mind only too well in his writings and, unlike most of his International style colleagues, he claimed to be anti-aesthetic, though he was not as we shall see anti-aesthetic in the same sense as Scharoun and Häring. But let the the man speak for himself.

All things in this world are a product of the formula function times economy. All art is composition and, hence, is unsuited to achieve goals. All life is function and is therefore unartistic ... In its design the new dwelling becomes not only a 'machine for living', but also a biological apparatus serving the needs of body and mind. The new age provides new building materials for the new way of building houses: (list of thirty building materials follows: reinforced concrete, aluminium, ripolin etc.) We organise these building materials into a con-

The staff canteen of the Berlin State library with exposed air conditioning ducts under the northlight roof.

structive whole based on economic principles. Thus the in-dividual shape, the body of the structure, the colour of the material and the surface texture evolve by themselves and are determined by life. Snugness and prestige are not leitmotivs for dwelling construction. The first depends on the human heart and not on the walls of a room, the second manifests itself in the manner of the host and not by his Persian carpet!

Architecture as 'an emotional act of the artist' has no justifi-cation. Architecture as 'a continuation of the traditions of building' means being carried along by the history of archi-tecture. This functional, biological interpretation of archi-tecture as giving shape to the functions of life, logically leads to pure construction: this world of constructive forms knows no native country. It is the expression of an international atti-tude in architecture. Internationality is a privilege of the period. Pure construction is the basis and the characteristic of the new world of forms.

1 sex life; 2 sleeping habits; 3 pets; 4 gardening; 5 personal hygiene; 6 weather protection; 7 hygiene in the home; 8 car maintenance; 9 cooking; 10 heating; 11 exposure to the sun; 12 service. These are the only motives when building a house. We examine the daily routine of everyone who lives in the house and this gives us the function-diagram for the father, the mother, the child, the baby and the other occupants. We explore the relationships of the house and its occupants to the world outside: postman, passer-by, visitor, neighbour, burglar, chimney-sweep, washerwoman, policeman, doctor, charwoman, playmate, gas inspector, tradesman, nurse and messenger boy, we explore the relation-ships of human beings and animals to the garden, and the interrelationships between human beings, pets and domestic insects. We determine the annual fluctuations in the tempera-ture of the ground and from that calculate the heat loss of the floor and the resulting depth required for the foundation blocks. The geological nature of the soil informs us about its capillary capacity and determines whether water will naturally drain away or whether drains are required ...[49]

Now Meyer might seem at first sight quite close to Häring. Like Häring he writes of 'building' as opposed to 'Architecture', and he believes that buildings should be generated according to functional considerations. But unlike Häring he thinks that all functions can be objectively defined: everything to do with a build-ing is to be measured, analysed and provided for. There is no room for any kind of superstitition or sub-jectivity: where what might be called 'aesthetic needs' are acknowledged at all they are subjected to the same kind of objective scrutiny as everything else, for where the engineer falls short the psychologist is supposed to take over. This is what might loosely be called the scientific attitude to architecture. It rests on an assumption that all architectural problems can be objectively defined and therefore solved and, in mak-ing this assumption, its adherents deny the existence of anything not measurable within their terms. They set up a finite system and then ignore everything out-side it.

Notice the way in which Meyer, after listing his twelve functions for a dwelling, insists that 'these are the only motives for building a house'. Now if Meyer's system was complete, if it was able to take into account the sum total of the effects of architecture, then we would be obliged to accept his as the correct attitude to design. But unfortunately only the rather more obvious functions of buildings are objectively measur-able and definable. We can measure the temperature of a room or the amount of light falling at a particular spot, we can measure how much noise gets through the partitions and how much water comes out of the taps, but we cannot measure the quality of a view or make any objective assessments about what buildings mean to people and how they identify with them. Psy-chologists can give us some hints about these things, but they are far from able to give us a complete and reliable analysis. 'But psychology is in its infancy', Meyer and his friends would argue. 'One day psycho-logists will have all the answers.' But will they?

Meyer's architectural philosophy is founded on the erroneous though widely held belief that science is the key to reality, a belief that is rooted in the nineteenth century but which scientists have rejected in the twen-tieth. Amedée Ozenfant described this state of mind and its limitations particularly well in his extraordi-nary book *Foundations of Modern Art* of '28, so I shall let him put the case for me.

Taken as a whole, the nineteenth century is an era given up to experiment. Everything that instruments can register is analysed: the results accumulate. There is a certainty in the air, that so remarkable a collection of facts must inevitably end by revealing the secret of the profoundest human prob-lems, and the why and the wherefore, the beginnings, the nature of existence, and above all, throw light on what may be beyond the grave ...

Today the deepest, most earnest men of science no longer attempt to explain. They realise that they are only observing in the world outside them, the world inside them, and perfect-ing means of doing so. Newton saw all bodies subject to the laws of gravity which he had formulated: Henri Poincaré worked over these laws and adapted them to modern findings, and asserted that the universe only appeared to be subject to them. Einstein introduces new modifications into a theory which tomorrow may prove untenable.

What in fact, are the resources of science? And by what detours is it able to supplement our limited senses? By arm-ing them with more responsive, more penetrating instru-ments? Yet the deeper world into which we thus penetrate is still perceived sensorially.

In the last resort, our reason, our logic, are human too. Science is incapable, therefore, of discovering anything irrational in our universe. And anything which should be so would pass unperceived by us, for we are so made as to be capable of perceiving only what is perceptible to us, which is the same as saying that our brains are rational. For that reason the universe must appear to us determined by definite laws, and science thus becomes possible. But all it does is to write the word 'thousand' over an already existent whole.

The ancients believed that only a mist, as it were, separated us from the reality of the universe, but we know now that this cloud cannot be resolved, and that, far from being a vapour to be dispersed by enlightenment, it is the armour-plating of the unknowable. Armour-plating? Every use of language is inappropriate, for we know nothing, and we but dupe ourselves with images. Metaphors all!

Our ineluctable darkness is but too apparent: neither science nor philosophy are able to give us any absolute certainty. They can register the relation between apparent facts and schematically group those which recur often, and only those: but never can they seize Reality as it is, and still less satisfy our ardent curiosity as to the nature of things or ourselves.

You hear people talk of the dramatic night of the middle ages, and compare it with the daylight that shines in our own age: but we know now that we know nothing: or yes, we know we can know nothing with certainty. The conception of the universe as something absolute has disappeared.[50]

The shift in scientific thinking that Ozenfant describes so well is of course the same shift that Häring considered so significant (p. 125). Interestingly, both men cite the discoveries of Einstein. There is no link between them, they came to similar conclusions because they were both aware of contemporary scientific thinking and its philosophical implications.

But I must get back to Meyer. My essential purpose in digressing was to prove that the psychologist will never have all the answers, that we shall never live in a tidy scientific world and that therefore the quest for totally rational design is a vain one. Meyer's approach fails because it depends on being complete and yet it never can be. Buildings designed according to the kind of strict rationalist principles he set out tend to work well at the level of obvious physical needs, but often fail to provide an environment which people find adequate at an emotional level because emotional needs are not considered, being undefinable. Meyer pretends they do not exist, but he is wrong, for contrary to his statements prestige *is* an important consideration in dwelling design and it manifests itself *both* in the manner of the host *and* in his Persian carpet.

In the city architecture surrounds us completely – almost our whole environment is made up of buildings, so they must affect us in almost every possible way and we must experience them at all levels. Thus not only are most of the effects of buildings on people indefinable, but they are almost infinitely numerous. How then can we work in such a situation?

Häring and Scharoun recognised the necessity of using all one's faculties in the design process. Measurable things could be measured and provided for rationally but unmeasurable things which could only be gauged emotionally or instinctively were handled in an inevitably subjective manner. The different faculties of the mind were like a set of specialised tools each carefully sharpened for a particular task and used with a particular skill. Both men stressed the importance of intuition, not a wild, uncontrolled intuition like that of the pure artist who serves only himself, rather a trained and disciplined intuition subservient to the task in hand. For of course, as I have stressed before, the outstanding feature of 'new building' is the belief that the architect is an interpreter rather than a creator, that he is the medium through which the task expresses itself. Surely Scharoun and Häring were right, for if we cannot be totally rational and objective then we have to be subjective, but we can at least be relevantly subjective.

Notes

1. F. L. Wright, *The Future of Architecture* (New York: Mentor Books 1963), p. 41.
2. Scharoun's address 'Raum and Milieu der Schule' at the International Congress of School Design, Mailand, 1960. Quoted in M. Staber, 'Scharoun, a Contribution to Organic Building', *Zodiac 10*, p. 75.
3. Scharoun, from his report on the theatre design for Kassel. Quoted in English in Hatje, Hoffmann and Kaspar, *New German Architecture* (London: Architectural Press 1956), p. 118.
4. Scharoun, from Kassel report. Quoted M. Staber, *Zodiac 10*, pp. 58–60.
5. Scharoun, from his report on the Philharmonie. Quoted in English in a publicity leaflet printed by Thormann and Goetsch, Berlin.
6. B. Taut, extract from a pamphlet about the exhibition of unknown architects organised by the Arbeitstrat für Kunst, Berlin, 1919. Quoted in English in Conrads and Sperlich, *Fantastic Architecture* (London: Architectural Press 1963), p. 138.
7. Circular quoted at length in U. Conrads, *Programmes and Manifestoes of Twentieth Century Architecture* (London: Lund Humphries, 1970), pp. 44–5.
8. A. Behne, 'Glass Architecture', written 1918 and published 1919 in *Wiederkehr der Kunst* (Leipzig: Kurt Wolff Verlag 1919). Quoted in English in Conrads and Sperlich, *Fantastic Architecture*, p. 32.
9. W. Gropius, extract from a pamphlet. Quoted in English in Conrads and Sperlich, *Fantastic Architecture*, p. 137.
10. B. Taut, extract from a circular letter of 1920. Quoted in English in Conrads and Sperlich, *Fantastic Architecture*, p. 148.
11. Scharoun, extract from a circular letter of 1919. Quoted in English in Conrads and Sperlich, *Fantastic Architecture*, p. 142.
12. Luckhardt, extract from a circular letter, undated. Quoted in English in Conrads and Sperlich, *Fantastic Architecture*, p. 144.
13. Le Corbusier, *Towards a New Architecture* (London: John Rodker, 1927), p. 29.
14. H. Häring, *Formulations Towards a Reorientation in the Applied Arts*, 1927. Quoted in English in Conrads, *Programmes and Manifestoes*, p. 103.
15. H. Häring, *Formulations*, 1927. Quoted in English in Conrads, *Programmes and Manifestoes*, p. 104.
16. H. Häring, *Wege zur Form*, 1925. Author's translation.
17. H. Häring, *Wege zur Form*, 1925. Author's translation.
18. H. Häring, *The House as an Organic Structure*, 1932. Quoted in English in Conrads, *Programmes and Manifestoes*, p. 126.
19. Idem., p. 127.
20. J. Ruskin, 'The Nature of Gothic', from *The Stones of Venice* (New York: John Wiley, 1884), p. 203.
21. H. Häring, 'The Problem of Art and Structure in Building'. Quoted in English in J. Posener, *From Schinkel to the Bauhaus* (London: Lund Humphries, AA Paper No. 5, 1972), p. 34.
22. C. Fiedler. Quoted in English in Herbert Read, *The Aesthetics of Architecture* (London: Professional Publications, AA 125, Commemorative Publication, 1973), pp. 176–80.
23. W. Worringer. Quoted in English in Herbert Read, *The Aesthetics of Architecture*.
24. A. W. Pugin, *The True Principles of Pointed or Christian Architecture* (London: Henry Bohn, 1853; reprinted Oxford: St Barnabas Press, 1969), p. 1.
25. Ibid., p. 43.
26. Ibid., pp. 51–2.
27. J. Ruskin, 'The Nature of Gothic', p. 178.
28. Ibid., p. 229.
29. Ibid., pp. 206–7.
30. Ibid., p. 207.
31. A. W. Pugin, *The True Principles of Pointed Architecture*, p. 52.
32. H. Muthesius, '*Das Englische Haus*'. Quoted in English in J. Posener, *From Schinkel to the Bauhaus*, p. 18.
33. Idem.
34. H. Van de Velde, 'Credo 1907'. Quoted in English in Conrads, *Programmes and Manifestoes*, p. 18.
35. H. Häring, *Wege zur Form*, 1925. Author's translation.
36. Scharoun, report on competition scheme. Quoted in English in Rosenberg, 'Berlin and the Haupstadt Berlin Competition', *Architects' Year Book No. 9* (London 1959), pp. 68–94.
37. Scharoun, from his report on the theatre design for Kassel, 1952. Quoted in English in Staber, *Zodiac 10*, p. 85.
38. Scharoun, 'Schiffahrtsmuseum Bremerhaven', *Bauwelt*, no. 34 (Germany, 1970), pp. 1307–8. Author's translation.
39. Mies van der Rohe, gramophone record (Bauwelt 1969).
40. A. W. Pugin, *The True Principles of Pointed Architecture*, p. 46.
41. R. Sommer, *Personal Space* (London: Spectrum Books 1969); see Chapter 7 – Designed for Learning, pp. 98–119.
42. P. Boulez, BBC radio interview (unpublished).
43. C. Fiedler. Quoted in English in Read, *Aesthetics of Architecture*, pp. 176–80.
44. H. Häring, 'The Problem of Art and Structure in Building'. Quoted in English in Posener, *From Schinkel to the Bauhaus*, p. 34.
45. W. Worringer, *Abstraction and Empathy* (Germany: 1908; English edition London: Routledge and Kegan Paul, 1953), pp. 15–17.
46. P. Blake, *Mies van der Rohe* (London: Pelican, 1963), p. 74.
47. Scharoun, extract from a circular letter, 1919.
48. H. Häring, 'The Problem of Art and Structure in Building'. Quoted in English in Posener, *From Schinkel to the Bauhaus*, p. 34.
49. H. Meyer, *Building*, 1928. Quoted in English in Conrads, *Programmes and Manifestoes*, pp. 117–20.
50. A. Ozenfant, *Foundations of Modern Art* (New York: Dover, 1952), pp. 173–5.

Bibliography

The serious student of Scharoun wishing to go beyond the scope of this book must study the German sources. He should go straight to the definitive monograph: *Hans Scharoun, Bauten, Entwürfe, Texte* edited by the late Peter Pfankuch and published by Gebr. Mann Verlag, Berlin, for the Akademie der Künste. This contains a complete list of works and a comprehensive list of references which are not reproduced here in full for lack of space.

The equivalent book on Hugo Häring, again only available in German, is *Hugo Häring – Schriften, Entwürfe, Bauten* edited by Jürgen Joedicke and Heinrich Lauterbach, and published by Karl Krämer Verlag, Stuttgart. This contains many of Häring's principal essays, photographs and plans of his few built works and reproductions of many sketches and drawings. The student with really fluent German should also tackle his *Fragmente* published by the Akademie der Künste in Berlin, which consists of his collected notes for an unwritten magnum opus on the derivation of form.

Readers limited to English will find very little material directly about Scharoun or Häring. Most general books on post-war German architecture contain the odd building or two by Scharoun with accompanying text. A general article entitled *Hans Scharoun, ein Betrag zum Organischen Bauen* by Margit Staber can be found in *Zodiac 10* of 1962 with a very bad English translation at the end, and for those who can read French the special edition of *Aujourd'hui L'Art et L'Architecture* of 1967, devoted to Germany, may be of some interest. It contains plans and photographs of several Scharoun buildings and projects, along with short essays by various critics.

Readers limited to English interested in exploring the Utopian period will find *Expressionist Architecture* by Wolfgang Pehnt published in English by Thames and Hudson the most detailed general source, while *Fantastic Architecture* by Conrads and Sperlich published in English by the Architectural Press contains many period documents. Ulrich Conrads also edited *Programmes and Manifestoes on 20th century Architecture*, published in English by Lund Humphries.

Those who wish to explore the background of New building and its relation with the Gothic Revival as expounded here in Chapters 7 and 8, will find the following books of particular interest: *Style and Society* by Robert Macleod, RIBA Press; *From Schinkel to the Bauhaus* by Julius Posener, AA Paper No. 5, Lund Humphries, 1972; *The True Principles of Christian or Pointed Architecture*, by A. W. Pugin, 1853, reprinted facsimile by St Barnabas Press, Oxford, 1969; *Abstraction and Empathy* by Wilhelm Worringer, 1908, English edition by Routledge and Kegan Paul, 1953; *Philip Webb and his Work* by W. R. Lethaby, OUP, 1935; *The Gothic Revival: Sources, Influences and Ideas*, by Georg Germann, Lund Humphries, 1972.

Complete List of Works

Many of Scharoun's buildings and projects were published in German periodicals which are available at major reference libraries. A complete list of periodical references can be found in the German monograph, but I have selected for each project the readily available periodical which covers it in most detail, and set these references alongside a translation of the complete list of architectural works which was compiled by the Akademie der Künste. The periodicals referred to are notated as follows:

AD   *Architectural Design*, London
AR   *Architectural Review*, London
AYB *Architects' Year Book*, London
B   *Bauwelt*, Berlin
DB   (pre-war) *Deutsche Bauzeitung*, Berlin
       (post-war) *Die Bauzeitung*, Stuttgart
NB   Neue Bauwelt, Berlin
SANZ *Stadtbaukunst alter und neuer Zeit*, Berlin
W   *Werk*, Winthertur, Switzerland

1 Church in Bremerhaven, 1911, competition project.
2 Plan for the Kaiser-Wilhelm-Platz in Geestemünde, 1913, competition project.
3 Kruchen house, Buch, near Berlin, 1913, with Paul Kruchen.
4 Freymuth Sanatorium, Babelsberg, near Berlin, 1913, with Paul Kruchen.
5 Grunewald Sanatorium, Grunewald, near Berlin, 1913, with Paul Kruchen, project.
6 Hospital in Mariendorf, near Berlin, 1914, with Paul Kruchen.
7 Community Hall, Angerburg, 1914, competition project.
8 Town planning scheme for Gumbinnen, East Prussia, 1915, project.
9 Temporary church in Walterkehmen, East Prussia, 1916, conversion of a riding-school.
10 Inn at Goldaper Lake, East Prussia, 1916, project.
11 Community Hall, Kattenau, East Prussia, 1917.
12 Farmhouse at Thierfeld, near Gumbinnen, East Prussia, 1917/18.
13 Housing development near Insterburg, East Prussia, 1918, semi-detached houses with stables.
14 State housing development in Insterburg, East Prussia, 1919, detached and semi-detached houses, terraces, and 4-flat blocks, project.
15 'Tivoli', Insterburg, East Prussia, 1919, conversion of a hall into a theatre, project.
16 Dortmund Cemetery, 1919, competition project. DB 1919, No. 97, p. 572.
17 Plan for the cathedral square at Prenzlau, 1919, competition project – 1st prize. SANZ 1920, No. 6, pp. 85–9.
18 Emmerich Town Hall, 1919, competition project.
19 Swimming baths, Prenzlau, 1919, competition project.
20 Pair of houses, Pregelstrasse, Insterburg, East Prussia, 1920.
21 Gutzeit house near Gumbinnen, East Prussia, 1920, conversion.
22 Kamswyken housing development near Insterburg, East Prussia, 1920.
23 Cultural centre, Gelsenkirchen, 1920, competition project. DB 1920, No. 43, p. 244.
24 Extension of industrial premises for the firm Matheus Müller, Eltville, Rheinhessen, 1920, competition project. DB 1920, No. 39, p. 228.
25 Town Hall and church square, Lyck, East Prussia, 1920, competition project.
26 Town planning scheme for Insterburg, East Prussia, 1920/21, competition project.
27 Post office at Bremen railway station, 1921, competition project.
28 Museum of Medicine, Dresden, 1920, competition project. DB 1920, No. 38, p. 224.
29 Plan for the new market at Insterburg, East Prussia, 1921, competition project – 1st prize.
30 Farmhouse, Santilten, East Prussia, 1921/22, conversion.
31 Farmyard with forge and riding stables, Kuinen, East Prussia, 1922.
32 Stock Exchange building, Königsberg, Prussia, 1922, competition project. DB 1922, No. 45, p. 280; No. 48, p. 300.
33 Chicago Tribune office building, 1922, competition project.
34 Multi-storey office building on Friedrichstrasse, Berlin, 1922, competition project, DB 1921, No. 97, p. 426; 1922, No. 15, pp. 89–91.
35 Granary at Wertheim, East Prussia, 1922.
36 Wesel Town Hall, 1922, competition project.
37 One-family houses, Insterburg, East Prussia, 1922.
38 Gobert house, Sodehnen, East Prussia, 1922.
39 Monument to Kant, Königsberg, Prussia, 1922, competition project.
40 Business premises and flats, Insterburg, East Prussia, 1923, conversion.
41 Three and four storey blocks of flats for rental, Parkring, Insterburg, East Prussia, 1923/24.
42 Buildings for the Prince Albrecht Gardens, Berlin, 1924, competition project.
43 Planning of the Münsterplatz, Ulm, 1924/25, competition project. B 1925, No. 7, pp. 125–32.
44 Public buildings at the Spa of Bad Mergentheim, Württemberg, 1924/25, competition project. DB 1926, No. 2, p. 11.
45 Business premises in Frankfurt, 1924/25, competition project.
46 House for Professor Siegel, Insterburg, East Prussia, 1925, project.
47 Tannenberg Monument, 1925, competition project. B 1925, No. 25, pp. 580–4.

48 Bochum Town Hall, 1925, competition project.

49 Konitzer shop, Marienburg, East Prussia, 1925, project.

50 Water-tower, 1925, competition project, three versions.

51 Bridgehead building, Cologne, 1925, competition design. DB 1921, No. 96, pp. 421–3; No. 97, p. 425; No. 98, p. 429.

52 Exhibition site and fairground, Berlin, 1927, competition project. DB 1928, No. 7, pp. 97–100.

53 Station square, Duisburg, 1926, competition project.

54 The elastic ground plan, 1926, variable dwellings for apartment blocks, project.

55 Pöpelwitz housing development, Breslau, 1926, competition project.

56 Town Hall, Insterburg, East Prussia, 1927, competition project.

57 Exhibition hall, Breslau, 1927, project, two versions.

58 Transportable wooden house for the German Garden and Industry exhibition, Liegnitz, 1927. DB 1927, No. 7, p. 78; No. 84, pp. 693–6.

59 One-family house at the Werkbund exhibition, Stuttgart-Weissenhof, 1927. DB 1927, No. 59, pp. 489–91; No. 76, pp. 625–31.

60 Replanning of the Ministergardens area, Berlin, 1927, town planning scheme also involving Behrens, Poelzig, Rading and Tessenow under the direction of Martin Wagner.

61 Offices and fire-station, Breslau, 1927, competition project. DB 1928, No. 1, pp. 1–10.

62 Extension to the Reichstag, Berlin, 1927, competition project, two versions. DB 1928, No. 3, pp. 33–43; No. 8, p. 87.

63 Swimming baths near the Zoo, Berlin, 1927, project.

64 Apartment block, Berlin-Dahlem, 1927, project.

65 Evangelical church, Breslau-Zimpel, 1928, competition project.

66 School, Breslau-Zimpel, 1928, competition project.

67 Apartment block for single people at the entrance to the Werkbund exhibition, Breslau, 1928, first project.

68 Civic hall and exhibition hall, Bremen, 1928, competition project. DB 1928, No. 9, pp. 113–24.

69 School buildings on Schlichtallee, Berlin-Lichtenberg, 1928, competition project.

70 One-family house, 1928, competition project.

71 Hotel, Wesermünde, 1928, project.

72 Monument to Richard Wagner, Leipzig, 1928, competition project.

73 Apartment block on the Kaiserdamm, Berlin-Charlottenburg, 1928/29. B 1929, No. 18, p. 428; 1932, No. 6, p. 153.

74 Housing, Kaiserstrasse, Bremerhaven, 1929.

75 Apartment block, Heidelberger Platz, Berlin-Wilmersdorf, 1929, project.

76 Apartment block, Paulsbornerstrasse, Berlin-Wilmersdorf, 1929, project.

77 Apartment block, Werkbund exhibition, Breslau, June–Sept 1929. Yorke and Gibberd, The Modern Flat, 1937, p. 159.

78 Exhibition pavilion, Desta, for German Iron and Steel Co, 1929, project.

79 Apartment block, Hohenzollerndamm 35/36, Berlin-Wilmersdorf, 1929/30. B 1932, No. 6, p. 3; AR 1934, No. 447, p. 41.

80 Law courts, Berlin, Invalidenstrasse, Berlin-Tiergarten, 1930, competition project.

81 Housing project, Siemensstadt, Berlin, 1930; site plan and blocks on Jungfernheideweg and Mäckeritzstrasse. B 1930, No. 46, pp. 1–24. Yorke and Gibberd, The Modern Flat, 1937, pp. 52, 60.

82 Apartment block, Lindner, Berlin, 1930, project.

83 Terraced housing, Schlachtensee type, 1930, project.

84 Terraced housing, Halensee type, 1930, project.

85 Monument to Richard Wagner, Leipzig, 1930, competition project.

86 Apartment block on Flinsberger Platz, Berlin-Wilmersdorf, 1931. (Burnt out in 1944 and rebuilt in 1963 by others).

87 Civic hall, Rostock, 1930, competition project.

88 Shop sign for the firm 'Leiser,' Berlin, 1931, project.

89 War memorial in Thüringer Wald, 1931, competition project.

90 Steinhausen house, Falkenhain, near Berlin, 1931, conversion project.

91 The contemporary house, 1931, competition project for Bauwelt. B 1931, No. 9, p. 34.

92 Housing Kottbusser Tor, Berlin-Kreuzberg, 1931, project.

93 Housing Treseburger Ufer, Berlin-Neukölln, 1931, project.

94 Housing Hauptstrasse, Berlin-Schöneberg, 1931, project.

95 Housing Kaiserdamm, Berlin-Charlottenburg, 1931, project.

96 'Wonolett', ground plan types, project.

97 Three one-family houses for Ferdinand Möller, Potsdam, 1931, project.

98 Apartment block with access galleries, Berlin, 1931, project.

99 One-family house, Löbau type, 1931, project.

100 Pair of semi-detached houses, 1931, project.

101 Suburban housing scheme, 1931, project, with Erwin Gutkind.

102 Housing and cinema, Spandauer Damm, Berlin-Charlottenburg, 1931, project.

103 Housing scheme, Berlin, 1931, 2-storey apartment blocks, project.

104 Flat plans for 4-storey apartment blocks, 1931, project.

105 Housing, Berlin-Wannsee, 1931, project.

106 Apartment block, Reichsstrasse, Berlin-Charlottenburg, 1931, project.

107 Flat plans for a central corridor block, 1931, project.

108 Apartment block, Hindenburgplatz, Bremerhaven, 1931, project.

109 One-family house, 1932, three versions, project.

110 Square building, 1932, flat plans, project.

111 The growing house, timber house at the exhibition 'Sun, Air and Houses for All', Berlin, 1932. B 1961, No. 41/42, pp. 1190–4.

112 Apartment block on Landsberger Allee, Berlin-Lichtenberg, 1932, project.

113 Cinema in Bremerhaven, 1932, project.

114 Panke-Park, park between Berlin-Wedding and Bernau, 1932, project.

115 The transportable house, 1932, varied ground plans, project.

116 Apartment block on Hohenzollernring, Berlin-Spandau, 1932.

117 Wenzeck house, Berlin-Frohnau, 1932.

118 Schuldenfrey house, Garystrasse 26, Berlin-Dahlem.

119 Apartment block with variable flats, 1932, project.

120 Apartment block, 1932, project.

121 One-family house with arcade, 1932, project.

122 Apartment block, Zweibrückerstrasse 38–46, Berlin-Spandau, 1933.

123 The variable dwelling, combination of single-person and family flats, 1933, project.

124 Schminke House, Löbau, Saxony, 1933. DB 1953, No. 5, p. 166. Yorke, The Modern House, 1962, p. 108.

125 Strauss House, Hüninger Strasse, Berlin-Dahlem, 1933.

126 Stockholm, town-planning scheme, 1933, competition project.

127 Apartment block, Alexanderplatz, Berlin, 1933, project.

128 Mattern House, Bornim, near Potsdam, 1933. B 1935, No. 12, pp. 3–5. Yorke, The Modern House, 1962, p. 140.

129 Loeser & Richter works, Löbau, Saxony, 1934, conversion and extension.

130 Group of one-family houses at Bürgerpark, Wesermünde, 1934, project.

131 Holiday houses for a hotel in Vietznau, Switzerland, 1934, project.

132 Shop for the mosaic works Müller-Oerlinghausen, Berlin-Charlottenburg, 1934. B 1961, No. 41/42, p. 1178.

133 House for Professor Gocht, 1934, project.

134 Baensch house, Berlin-Spandau, Höhenweg 9, 1935.

135 Hoffmeyer house, Bremerhaven, Friesenstrasse 6, 1935.

136 Small housing project, Kladow-Hottengrund, Berlin, 1933.

137 Pflaum house, Falkensee, near Berlin, 1935.

138 Housing, Kaiserstrasse 224–38, Bremerhaven, 1936.

139 House, Berlin-Heiligensee, 1936.

140 Moll house, Berlin-Grunewald, 1936, destroyed 1944.

141 Housing, Elbestrasse, Bremerhaven, 1937.

142 Möller house, Zermützelsee, near Altruppin, Brandenburg, 1937.

143 Biskupski house, Zermützelsee, near Altruppin, Brandenburg, 1938.

144 Housing, Blessmannstrasse, Bremerhaven, 1938.

145 Krüger house, Berlin-Nikolasse, 1938, Rehwiese 4, conversion.

146 Bonk house, Bornim, near Potsdam, 1938.

147 Housing, Humboldstrasse, Berlin-Reinickendorf, 1938, project.

148 Just house, Berlin-Schlachtensee, 1938, project.

149 Noack house, near Potsdam, 1937/38.

150 Block of 8 flats, Yorkstrasse, Bremerhaven, 1938, conversion project.

151 Weidhaas house, Leipzig, 1939, project, two versions.

152 Garden bath-house for Silbermann family, Brandenburg/Havel, 1939.

153 Scharf house, Berlin-Schmargendorf, Miquelstrasse 39A & B, 1939.

154 Mohrmann house, Berlin-Lichtenrade, Falkensteinstrasse 10, 1939.

155 Housing, Kaiserstrasse, 240–54, Bremerhaven, 1940.

156 Endell house, Berlin-Wannsee, Kleinen Wannsee 30B, 1940.

157 Studio-conversion, Kantstrasse 12, Berlin-Charlottenburg, 1940.

158 Central Laundry, research project, 1941–3.

159 Weigand house, Borgsdorf, near Berlin, 1942.

160 Müller-Oerlinghausen house, Kressbronn/Bodensee, 1943, conversion.

161 Möller house (142), extension, 1943.

162 Berlin Plan by Planungskollektiv group, 1946. NB 1948, No. 10, pp. 147–52. AYB 1959, pp. 68–94.

163 Plastic House, Type Deutschland 1946, with Karl Böttcher, project and model.

164 Exhibition gallery at Friedrichstrasse station, Central Berlin, 1946, project.

165 Wilhelm house, Berlin-Kladow, 1948, project.

166 America house, Bremerhaven, 1948, conversion.

167 Exhibition gallery for Gerd Rosen, 1948, project.

168 Opera House, Leipzig, 1949, competition project.

169 Cellulose factory, Magdeburg, Rothensee, 1949, project.

170 Housing (neighbourhood unit), Berlin-Friedrichshain, 1949, site plan and buildings, project.

171 Liederhalle (small concert hall), Stuttgart,

1949, competition project, 1st prize but unexecuted.

172 German Academy of Sciences, Institute of Building, Central Berlin, Hannoversche Strasse 30, 1949, conversion.

173 Schminke house, extension, 1950, project.

174 Shops and apartments, Kurfürstendamm 182, Berlin-Charlottenburg, 1950, project.

175 Primary school, Darmstadt, 1951, project. DB 1951, No. 10, pp. 411–20. B 1960, No. 37, pp. 1075–7.

176 American Memorial Library, Berlin Kreuzberg, Blücherplatz, 1951, competition, 2nd prize. NB, 1951, No. 51, p. 826.

177 Heinrich-Mendelssohn building, Kaiserdamm, Berlin-Charlottenburg, 1952, competition project.

178 Siemensstadt Centre, Jungfernheideweg, 1952, project.

179 High-rise block, Siemensstadt, 1952, project.

180 Kassel Theatre, 1952, competition project, 1st prize. B 1952, No. 44, pp. 173–80.

181 Kassel Theatre, revised project (unexecuted). DB 1953, No. 2, pp. 49–57.

182 Old people's home, Tiergarten, Berlin, 1952, competition project, 1st prize (unexecuted). NB 1952, No. 36, p. 575.

183 Heligoland development, 1952, competition project. B 1957, No. 9, pp. 193–201.

184 Experimental houses, Heligoland, 1953, project.

185 National theatre, Mannheim, 1953, competition project. DB 1953, No. 6, pp. 207–12.

186 Theatre, Gelsenkirchen, 1954, competition project.

187 'Romeo and Juliet' housing, Stuttgart-Zuffenhausen, 1954–9. B 1961, No. 21, pp. 599–607.

188 Private school, Bergneustadt, 1955, competition project.

189 Office building, Hannover, 1955, competition project.

190 New market, Hamburg Hammerbrook, 1955, competition project. B 1962, No. 47, p. 1312.

191 Marl, Westphalia, 1955, planning advice.

192 Restaurant, Hansaviertel, Berlin, 1955, project.

193 Administrative buildings for the firm 'Wella', Darmstadt, 1955, competition project, two versions.

194 Stroeher house, Darmstadt, 1955, project.

195 Housing, Siemensstadt, Goebelstrasse 1–9, 1955, extension to a block by Bartning.

196 Housing, North-Charlottenburg, Berlin, 1956–61, overall plan and several blocks of flats. B 1962, No. 15/16, pp. 399–415.

197 Bürgerweide Bremen, 1956, town planning competition project, 1st prize.

198 Orphanage, Stuttgart-Botnang, 1956, project.

199 Krupp Convent, Essen, competition project.

200 General plan for the Hansaviertel development, Berlin-Tiergarten, 1956, project.

201 One-family houses, Hansaviertel, Berlin-Tiergarten, 1956, project. B 1957, No. 42, p. 1123.

202 Concert hall for the Berlin Philharmonic, 1956, Berlin-Wilmersdorf, Bundesallee 1, competition project, 1st prize. B 1957, No. 4, pp. 76–80.

203 School at Holterhöfchen, Hilden, Westphalia, 1957, competition project.

204 Geschwister Scholl secondary school, Lünen, Westphalia, 1956–62. B 1960, No. 37, pp. 1069–83.

205 Civic hall, Bremen, 1957, competition project.

206 Concert hall, Saarbrücken, 1958, competition project, 3rd prize.

207 Shopping centre, Goebelplatz, North-Charlottenburg, Berlin, 1957, project.

208 Spandau old town, Berlin-Spandau, 1958, town planning project.

209 Rothenburg house, Berlin-Dahlem, 1958, conversion project.

210 State Savings Bank, Stuttgart, 1958, sketches.

211 Town Hall, Marl, Westphalia, 1958, competition project, 2nd prize. B 1958, No. 14, pp. 315–27.

212 Berlin as capital city, 1958, town planning competition project, 2nd prize. AYB 1959, pp. 68–94.

213 Reeperbahn–Millerntor, Hamburg, 1959, town planning project.

214 School, Marl, Westphalia, 1961–8. B 1961, No. 7, p. 163.

215 Studio flat plans, Berlin, project, 1960.

216 School for Social Studies, Linz, Austria, 1961, competition project.

217 'Salute' high-rise block, Stuttgart, 1961–3. B 1964, No. 35, pp. 951–7.

218 Hostel for students of foreign aid programmes, 1962, project.

219 'Leere Vasen' housing project, Böblingen, near Stuttgart, 1962.

220 Du Mont Schauberg publishers' offices, Cologne, 1962, project.

221 Dom-Römerberg-Bereich, Frankfurt, 1963, competition project, 3rd prize. B 1963, No. 34, pp. 960–77.

222 Concert hall for the Berlin Philharmonic orchestra, Kemperplatz, Berlin-Tiergarten, 1963 (completion). B 1964, No. 1/2, pp. 11–46. AD 1965, No. 3, pp. 113–28.

223 Re-planning of Mehringplatz, Berlin-Kreuzberg, 1963, competition project, 1st prize. B 1966, No. 41, p. 1135.

224 Neven-Du Mont house, Cologne, 1964, project.

225 Concert hall, Pforzheim, 1964, competition project.

226 Theatre, Zürich, 1964, competition project. W 1964, No. 12, pp. 439–48.

227 BP Offices, Hamburg, 1964, competition project. DB 1964, No. 10, pp. 771–4.

228 State library for the Institute of Prussian Culture, Berlin-Tiergarten, 1964, competition project, 1st prize. B 1964, No. 40/41, pp. 1068–73.

229 Theatre, Wolfsburg, 1965, competition project, 1st prize. B 1966, No. 19, pp. 534–7. AR 1975, March.

230 Housing, Rauhe Kapf, Böblingen, near Stuttgart, 1965. DB 1967, No. 5, p. 357.

231 Tormann house, Bad Homburg v.d. Höhe, 1966.

232 Faculty of Architecture, Berlin Technical University, 1966. B 1965, No. 23, p. 668.

233 Chapel of St John, Glockengarten, Bochum, 1966.

234 Church of the Transfiguration of Christ, Viktoria-Luise-Platz, Berlin-Schöneberg, 1966, project.

235 Art centre and hostel, Matthäikirchplatz, Berlin-Tiergarten, 1966, project. B 1968, No. 38, p. 1214.

236 State library Berlin, revised project, 1967–78. B 1967, No. 41, pp. 1015–21.

237 'Red garage', Stuttgart-Zuffenhausen, 1968.

238 Köpke house, Berlin-Dahlem, Im Dol 10, 1968.

239 Housing, Hasenbergsteige, Stuttgart, 1969, project.

240 Church and parish centre, Wolfsburg-Rabenberg, 1970.

241 Kindergarten, Wolfsburg-Detmerode, 1970.

242 High-rise block on the Zabel-Krüger-Damm, Berlin-Reinickendorf, 1970. B 1973, No. 33, p. 1439. AR 1975, March.

243 AOK Headquarters building, Mehringplatz, Berlin-Kreuzberg, 1970. B 1966, No. 41, p. 1135.

244 German Maritime Museum, Bremerhaven, 1970–5. B 1970, No. 34, p. 1307, AR 1976, March.

245 High-rise block 'Orplid', Böblingen, near Stuttgart, 1971.

246 Chamber music hall at the Philharmonie, Berlin-Tiergarten, 1971, to be executed.

247 State Institute for Musical Research, and Museum of Musical Instruments at the Philharmonie, Berlin-Tiergarten, 1971, to be executed.

249 German Embassy, Brasilia, 1963–71. DB 1969, No. 8, p. 604.

250 Theatre, Wolfsburg, (completion) 1973. B 1973, No. 34, p. 1489. AR 1975, March.

Index